The Place Just Right

The Place Just Right

An unexpected return to a small-town past

Brenda Baumhart Mezz

© 2017 Brenda Baumhart Mezz
All rights reserved.

ISBN-13: 9781982099237
ISBN-10: 1982099232

Dedication

To my mother, Helyn, teacher and poet, whose simple gifts I am only now beginning to appreciate. And to all my other teachers as well. Their lessons are reflected in every page of this book.

Hope Chest

Where are the sheets, the hemstitched pillow cases,
The quilts my mother pieced by hand for me,
Doilies embroidered fine, and edged with laces,
The linen napkins daintily used at tea?
I'm sure that once I laid them in this chest
As tenderly as now I move my child
When she's asleep. I had the very best
Sunbonnet and apron patterns styled
And tested by my grandmother. Now I find
Only a few frayed towels and tarnished spoons.
I want to give my child a light, the kind
Sun gives, a spirit bright as seven moons,
A snowflake voice, a pulley strung with ropes
To lift her starward, and a chest of hopes.

HELYN HECATHORN, 1939

Table of Contents

Part I · 1
Prologue · 3
The Alpha Garden Club · 8
With a Still Heart · 11
Wednesday Afternoon and Pattern-Book Paper Dolls · · · · · · · · · · · · · · 13
Time Capsule · 16
The Alpha Garden Club: Barriers · · · · · · · · · · · · · · · · · · 21
Eaton High School, Class of 1957 · · · · · · · · · · · · · · · · · 25
My Father's World · 29
Angel Flight: An After-Christmas Story · · · · · · · · · · · · · 32
Uncle Daisy · 37
Charley · 41
Baumhart's Drugstore · 45
Vermilion Redux · 50
Values in Transition · 55
Faith of My Grandfathers · 58
Shadow Memories · 62
Losing My Religion · 67
Provincial · 70

Part II · 75
The Alpha Garden Club Visits a Cemetery · · · · · · · · · · 77
Worth Doing · 80
Class Reunion · 83

Ajax	86
Grill Girls and the Sixties	90
Senioritis	97
Riding the Freeway	99
Theater	103
Jumping In	108
Peter Pan	114
Moving to L.A.	121
Not For Profit	124
San Fernando	127
Home Again	130
Lakengren	133
The Eaton Place	136
Part III	141
Nice to Remember	143
Jon	145
A Eulogy	150
Wrestling with Zeus	154
Comedy	158
Nycticorax Nycticorax	160
Two Thanksgivings	164
Ole Man Sorrow	170
Pollywog	175
Tellin' Me I'm Ole Now	180
Family	187
BJ and the Baptists	191
The Alpha Garden Club Christmas Meeting	196
Time and Variations	200
Acknowledgments	205
About the Author	207

Part 1

'TIS THE GIFT TO BE SIMPLE
'TIS THE GIFT TO BE FREE

'TIS THE GIFT TO COME DOWN
WHERE WE OUGHT TO BE

AND WHEN WE FIND OURSELVES
IN THE PLACE JUST RIGHT
IT WILL BE IN THE VALLEY
OF LOVE AND DELIGHT

"Simple Gifts"
A traditional Shaker hymn

Prologue

I never intended to return to Eaton, Ohio. When I was eighteen, I couldn't wait to leave. Over the years, my life moved as a pebble moves water—in constantly widening circles, lapping the shores of ever larger and more exciting places. Places to stimulate my mind, challenge my mettle, broaden my vistas. I forgot where I came from. I rarely thought about Ohio, never visited. Then two things happened: First, my mother—my lithe, limber, sensual, athletic mother—got old; second, I realized that one day soon, so would I.

My mother, bless her heart, was a victim of Alzheimer's disease, that most feared and frustrating of conditions. One minute she lived in Florida, tanned and swimming every day. She sounded just fine on the phone or when we went for the occasional visit. A little forgetful, perhaps. It happens to everyone, doesn't it? The next thing I knew, she had broken her leg while opening the curtains one morning, and even worse, was totally confused. We thought the confusion might clear as the leg healed. It didn't. So I brought her to Los Angeles, where I then lived, feeling guilty every minute I had neither the time nor the space to care for her personally.

I placed her first in an assisted-living facility. After a year, when she had begun roaming the halls at night knocking on people's doors, I moved her to an apartment with a full-time caretaker. I did this because facilities designed for Alzheimer's patients—locked down, malodorous, wheelchairs lined up against colorless walls and wraiths of former human beings wandering about dragging catheter bags—made my stomach roll and my heart scream. I visited several times a week bringing groceries, prescriptions, and whatever I thought might amuse her.

Brenda Baumhart Mezz

My gymnastic mother, Helyn Hecathorn, performing on the beach at Cedar Point, Ohio, circa 1937.

I watched her life from the latest years to the earliest peel away, layer by layer, into oblivion. She had spent her last twenty-five years in Florida, all except the last five with my stepfather, who died first. That place and relationship were the first to go. Year by year, decade by decade, it all slid away until she was left with the plea, "Please take me home!" And what home did she mean? The first one, of course. The house at 824 North Maple Street in Eaton, Ohio, where both she and I grew up, and where her father had brought her mother as a bride almost a century before. A home that she believed, in her confusion, was still her refuge, inhabited by a mother and father long dead and by the comfort and security she so desperately craved.

After she died, I took her home. She went to rest in the family plot at Roselawn Cemetery, in Lewisburg, a few miles from Eaton next to her parents and, incredibly, both sets of grandparents, as well as a dozen or so other relatives whose stones I found I could still identify without even stooping to read the names. In that moment going home became a possibility for me as well. I don't want to die like my mother in a strange place, isolated from my deepest images and rooted memories. The last memories to go. I am fortunate this place still exists. For many of my rootless generation, such a home can no longer be found on the map.

People say to me, "I'll bet Eaton has changed a lot since you lived here before."

"On the contrary," I answer. "I'm amazed it has changed so little."

In Marion Zimmer Bradley's *The Mists of Avalon*, three different eras of British life coexist in the same geographical space. The England of medieval Christianity and King Arthur's court appears on the surface obscuring, but not replacing, the earlier pagan Britain of the Druids. At the same time, the ancient, magical Britain of the fairies peers out in glimpses. In a supernatural realm of former lives, characters from different historical and mythological ages meet. In a far less mystical manner, the same is true of my hometown.

On the western edge of Ohio, Eaton, the contemporary village, is wired to the rest of the modern world through the Internet. Children appear on streets in the same trendy fashions found in California or New York City. Yet, at the Famous Preble County Fair last July, I was not surprised to find a group of children huddled in hot, dusty stalls in buildings decades old, brushing their hogs and goats, watering their roosters and rabbits. Their fresh faces peered out from simple haircuts, and they were dressed in the same worn jeans and blue Future Farmers of America jackets worn fifty or more years ago by their grandparents.

True, the fair features currently popular musical groups at the grandstand some nights, but they will be followed on other nights by traditional harness racing, sheep shearing, or tractor pulling. The mid-twentieth-century world of church suppers and high-school sports mania, of garden clubs, quilting, and meetings at the Grange Hall—the world I remember as a child—is still there, viable, visible without even scratching beneath the surface.

In downtown Eaton, as I pass the corner of Main and Barron Streets, I am often confronted by the nineteenth century as well. Living and breathing in prayer caps and caped, long dresses, crossing Barron Street to the post office in beards, round black hats, and overalls, the Dunkards go about their business. For as long as there has been an Eaton, the Dunkards, German Baptist Brethren, have resided here. They are farmers, mostly, with lives that hearken back to the days of pioneers, evoking a past still present in the barns and farmhouses along country roads and in the stubborn strength with which they face a new world—adapting where necessary, but uncompromising in their faith and determination to persist.

German Baptists often create eerie moments of juxtaposition between past and present, as in the case of the young employee at McDonald's who, when required to wear the company uniform, had obviously had one made for her in the familiar McDonald's color, but with long skirt and cape. She sat at the window at the drive-through handing out bags of Quarter Pounders and french fries, prayer cap covering the twisted bun of her uncut hair, personifying the blend of past and present found in my hometown.

Small towns dot the map all over America, miniature clusters of lights seen at night from a passing plane. Over the years as my husband, Jon, and I traveled from Los Angeles to his family in New York, I would look down over Ohio and wonder if that small illumination to the right, or the next one drifting over the unseen horizon, could be Eaton—my small town. It was impossible to tell from the sky; all the clusters looked similar. And there probably isn't much difference on the ground either whichever town it is, whatever the name.

The Place Just Right

Each town has a courthouse and a Main Street where local folks conduct business. Streets downtown are lined with two-story brick buildings, the names of the first owners and a date, maybe 1887, displayed somewhere on the top floor. Many these days are vacant or house law offices or insurance agencies instead of the retail establishments for which they were originally intended. A high school with a gym and a nearby football field and baseball diamond sits importantly on the outskirts of town. Except in summer, the town gathers on Friday nights at one game or another, events there providing conversation for the entire week to follow.

These are towns with tree-laden streets and backyards with swing sets and storage sheds for lawn mowers, abandoned tricycles, and Dad's tools. Somewhere the Little League Park sits surrounded by bleachers; also ubiquitous are diners serving chicken fried steak and pork chops for Sunday dinner after church. On a nicer side of town, among graceful, older homes, a country club and golf course create a swath of green. Somewhere else railroad tracks cut through run-down neighborhoods, and near them—a saloon. A fairground, maybe a Grange Hall or an auction barn, or perhaps a grain elevator sprawl at a place where town eases into country.

Barns, silos and endless fields—green, brown, or white, as the season dictates—surround the town for miles. The air is fresh, the nights full of stars. Robins appear in spring and fireflies at twilight in mid-summer; children leap into the community swimming pool, fingers tightly pinching noses as they drop squealing into blue water.

The small town in America is a cliché and a legend, a fact of life and a figment of the imagination. It has been the incubator for the best America has in values and generosity and a crucible of provincialism and ignorance—all at the same time. It is good to be back.

The Alpha Garden Club

On Saturday, September 15, 2001, the *Register-Herald* of Eaton, Ohio, carried a brief article on the September 4 meeting of the Alpha Garden Club. In spite of the world-changing events of September 11, the twice-weekly paper ran the item as planned. I was delighted because I had attended the meeting as a guest of Rosalie Kramer Unger, hostess and former high-school classmate, a fact duly noted in the article. It marked my debut, of sorts, into the larger social life of my old hometown.

It is heartening that in Eaton, news concerning meetings of the ladies is not bumped for major world events, as were professional football games and awards ceremonies. Respect for horror and destruction and for the courage that follows is appropriate. But life must persist. In a small town, much of that life is in the charge of ladies like those in the Alpha Garden Club, in existence since 1924.

My mother was not a "joiner," as she often proudly stated. Whether that was because of a quasi-intellectual impatience with the level of conversation at such clubs, resentment from a woman who had to work for a living rather than enjoy the comfortable domesticity of most women in those days, or a fear of being gossiped about as someone who "kept company" with a Catholic man she couldn't marry, I haven't decided. It was probably a combination of all three. But as a consequence, I didn't join clubs either.

I first got an inkling of the importance of women's gatherings in a small town from Helen Hooven Santmyer's sprawling novel *...And Ladies of the Club*, set in a fictional town not far from Eaton. She spent more than half her life writing it. By the time it was published, she was finishing out her days, hopefully with a great sense of accomplishment.

The Place Just Right

The book follows the lives of a group of women from just after the Civil War well into the twentieth century. These were women I recognized, women I had seen all my life—wives, fulfilled or desperately unhappy, or spinsters, many teachers, looking for a way to accept and find contentment in their lonely lot, both envying and pitying their married sisters. In the small Ohio town described in *...And Ladies of the Club*, the company of women was the most nourishing and dependable feature of every life there, year after year, crisis after crisis. So I attended the Alpha Garden Club, hoping to take a hesitant step into the lives of women in Eaton. Hoping to find a welcome. I was not disappointed.

I had a little trouble finding the old Kramer farm where the Alpha Garden Club was to meet, but after a few false turns at wrong lanes, my old homing sense came to life, and I finally recognized it through fields of maturing corn and soybeans, against a background of woods in the distance.

As I approached the old house where I had stayed overnight many times as a girl, I found a meal spread under trees on long tables, and about twenty women, mostly middle-aged, milling about admiring the flowers, talking in small groups. They looked at me with curiosity. It might have been awkward, and indeed was a little, until Rosalie explained who I was, and more important, who my mother was. Many of the women present remembered her as their high school English teacher, and for a woman who had not been a "joiner," she would have been amazed to know how affectionately she was regarded.

I had heard the same memories shared by others at her funeral—how well she taught them language, how, decades later, they still kept the notebooks made in her class. "Besides," one of the women said, "she was lively and different." They had loved the fact that she was small with a dancer's figure, wore very high heels in a variety of colors and styles, and sat on the edge of her desk, legs crossed. A stark contrast to the stodgy, corseted teachers in dark rayon dresses who made up the majority of the female faculty in those days. It was lovely to hear such things about my mother.

After a meal of bratwurst, sauerkraut, German potato salad, and homemade pie, the program began. Grace Rust, ninety-two years old and president for the past sixteen years, shared her "bad" day. She had lost her glasses for over an hour and finally found them only to discover that her dog had chewed up the pillows in the guest room, leaving feathers all over the bed and the floor. She passed around Polaroid pictures of the destroyed pillows, the dog, and the feathers. She then introduced the other officers. Kate Brown, also past ninety, read quite expertly some surprisingly suggestive riddles and jokes. I inquired of the people at the table exactly what her office was. "Chaplain," they replied, wryly.

Next, all of us, with help from Rosalie's husband, Jay, and with varying degrees of difficulty, climbed aboard a wagon and sat on bales of hay as a tractor pulled us through the one-hundred-acre woods. I visited with ladies on either side as we slowly bumped past beech, oak, and walnut trees. They spontaneously started singing "Way down yonder in the pawpaw patch" as we passed an enormous pawpaw tree covered with fruit.

Afterward, driving home, I was reminded how luxurious it must feel to live in the country, surrounded by nothing but fields, gardens, and woods; blissfully quiet, serenely peaceful, extravagantly private. I thought of English nobles on country estates. I remembered reading how great composers or poets would retreat to such estates to create masterpieces in the romantic solitude of sprawling lawns and bridle paths.

In an increasingly populated nation where living space is becoming more and more at a premium, rural life, once perceived as lonely, culturally deprived, overworked, and hardscrabble, is changing its face. City dwellers now romanticize "country living" with interior decoration and with yuppie preoccupations such as organic and gourmet gardening. Already, in some sections of Preble County, old farmhouses have been restored, not by original family members such as my friend Rosalie, but by strangers from the city. In the forty years since I left, my hometown and the surrounding countryside have changed very little. That may not be true about the next ten.

In the meantime, I have joined the Alpha Garden Club, paying $1.50 yearly dues and receiving an embroidered cloth booklet with the names and addresses of all the current members as well as a list of the past officers since 1924. I look forward to the next meeting. I want to taste as much as I can of small-town life just in case it disappears while I am looking the other way.

With a Still Heart

"Above all Siddhartha learned from the river how to listen, to listen with a still heart, with a waiting, open soul, without passion, without desire, without judgments, without opinions."—Hermann Hesse, *Siddhartha*, about the river by which Siddhartha sat in his later years, and which became his teacher.

When I was young, listening to anything with a still heart was incomprehensible. The stream of life, unlike Siddhartha's river, was meant to be leaped into, preferably naked, so the rushing water could create the maximum sensation. If there was music, I wanted to sing and dance; if there was color, I wanted to paint. It was never enough to be a passive observer, especially when there was a compelling spectacle. Now I am no longer young, and I am beginning to understand the immense satisfactions of listening and watching. I also understand, if only in glimpses, the much-to-be-desired concept of a "still heart."

Not long ago CBS in conjunction with the U.S. Open tennis tournament aired a feature on tennis competitions for eighty- and ninety-year-olds. The geezer padding around swatting at the ball at ninety-seven looked a lot like my memory of eighty-year-olds, while the eighty-year-olds, some still lunging for balls out of reach, seemed pretty darned competent by comparison. These venerable athletes were clearly not sitting by a stream watching for revelations from the light on the rippling water.

It is apparently not fashionable these days, nor considered particularly healthy, for old people to plop down with relief in the rocking chair and watch the world go by. We have learned what the ancient Greeks always knew: that physical and mental activity are more interrelated than supposed. As one weakens, so does the other. This translates into the notion that if part of my day is to be spent nurturing the life of the mind, I had better spend another substantial part of my day physically active in order to keep the mental faculties perking. After all, even Siddhartha spent much of his time rowing people back and forth across the river. His diet was spare, and his body lean and healthy.

But passive or active, or some of each, it seems appropriate, even imperative, as I get older to "examine" my life. And what better vantage point for such an endeavor than the place where most of my memories began? Unlike Siddhartha, I do not remain on the riverbank. I move through the panorama of my own past. As I drive along the streets of Eaton, the memories take me by surprise, summoned to mind by a familiar old building, a crooked tree at the corner of the school, or the mist-shrouded football field I happen on with a gasp of delight, having forgotten it is just around the corner ahead.

Sometimes, as I travel through town behind a windshield of glass and the armor of Mozart from my radio, everything appears miniaturized like the buildings and trees constructed for his Lionel trains by a man who is still a boy at heart. I think I could step out of my car and move everything around—rearrange the town to my liking.

Frequently, I visit 824 North Maple Street and stop for lively conversation with my feisty uncle Ben, who at eighty-eight and widowed, still lives in the old family home. I sit under the tree that cooled my summer nights when I was a girl, locate the stone that marked my secret place, the ancient grapevine miraculously still there. I remember the apple trees I loved to climb, the victory garden stretching to the alley, and seem to see once more my grandmother, head scarf tied beneath her chin, stooping over the tomato plants.

Beyond the streets of Eaton, deeply hidden in the plain/pretty Midwestern faces of the people I meet, in the flat/hearty speech typical of Preble County, lie more passages to the closets in my mind where, long neglected like old boxes in the attic, relics of my childhood lie hidden. Now I will open those boxes, the ones with peeling masking tape, marked crudely in black, covered with dust that rises and resettles on my hands and clothing. I am looking for the images of the past, the smells and textures, the music and colors, and for the tears and laughter that followed and left their mark. I want to recall how it felt when I jumped headfirst into that stream—this time watching and listening as well, with a still heart, to see what I can learn.

Wednesday Afternoon and Pattern-Book Paper Dolls

If I lived long enough in Ohio, it was inevitable that a true Wednesday afternoon would come along. My Wednesday afternoon—not the ones the calendar announces every month on a straight line down the middle. In my private world when I was a girl, days were designated not by calendars but by the moods they typically created. We all know what Monday morning feels like. But the feeling is not necessarily confined to Monday. In fact, Monday morning could even feel like Saturday night if it were festive enough. To this child at least, these feelings were more meaningful than the booklet with pictures of cows or kittens hanging by a nail on the kitchen wall at 824 North Maple Street.

Today was Wednesday afternoon, especially in the morning when it rained. And it called up a rush of images that have occupied my thoughts all day.

I see a small stranger in pigtails, dark brown hair pulled tightly from the middle sporting oversize bows. She is wearing a blue gingham dress tied by a sash at the back, sensible, ugly brown shoes with special arch supports, and a thoughtful look on her face. She is seated on a cushion on the floor by the parlor window studying the drops of rain as they collect on the windowpane. Outside the occasional car creates an ascending then descending swish as it travels the wet street. The room is comfortably gloomy here reflecting only the weak light of the sky. She is alone.

Grandma Nina is taking a nap, so it is important the house be quiet. Nothing is planned; it is nobody's birthday. Lunch was long ago, and supper is hours away. Time stretches in both directions, and it is all hers. Every gray, rain-echoing moment of it. For others, it is a discardable day—middle-of-the-week boring, dispensable. For the child left to her own devices, it is special—Wednesday afternoon.

Much can be learned by watching raindrops on the windowpane. Most are merely part of the crowd, pitched there by an aggressive wind, helpless and passive, scattered randomly over the glass. Others seem destined to be playground bullies, creeping downward, sucking up the liquid substance of the rest as they pass in multiple directions. The little scientist observes them swelling to monstrous proportions until, thrown off course by the enormous weight of their ingested victims, they plummet downward toward the sill to run off in a stream and be absorbed into the puddle forming at the base of the house. From there, of course, they will all be rushed to the gutter, down the sewer, and eventually, Sevenmile Creek. There, having long since lost any individuality, they will be sent back to the sky through evaporation and born again. But none of these karmic implications are yet imagined. For now, on Wednesday afternoon, the short trip down the pane is lesson enough.

When the survival-of-the-fittest battle of the raindrops has lost its allure, the little girl I once was will eagerly climb the steep stairs to the second floor, enter the big old-fashioned bathroom, and, stooping, make her way through a tiny door into a miniature playroom under a windowed gable at the front of the house to play paper dolls. It is similar to the children of Narnia entering their own world through the back of a wardrobe. For a child, other worlds are accessible through such mundane passages. That is, if they are left often enough to their own devices—and if it is Wednesday afternoon.

The playroom is just the right size for her. No adult could stand upright, but she can if she stays in the middle of the room where the gable rises to a peak. But mostly she sits, legs crossed, spreading the paper personages out before her on the floor. They are by now old friends, happy to be freed from their boxes and eager to be guided through another adventure by their mysterious, life-giving giant. The dolls are a large, motley assortment of figures never designed to be toys, but delighted to play the role. They have been selected and clipped from a pattern book, a huge Simplicity or Butterick collection of designs for clothes to be made at home—a book that once spent its life attached by a chain to a huge counter in the back of a fabric store, now donated by request of some ingenious adult to this little girl.

In a pattern book, some models are drawn to face left, others to face right, and a few, very few, straight on. Therefore, the world of my paper dolls divided into two camps, the right-facing people and the left-facing. Each of these two clans was headed by a matriarch—one by the haughty Rena in her two-piece bathing suit; the other by the more modest Serafina in shorts and halter top.

Rena was a force to be reckoned with. She stood proudly, her chin upraised, chest thrust forward, hand resting securely on her hip, tossing her reddish-blonde ringlets as if to say, "See how gorgeous I am?" Serafina was more retiring, peeking at the world coyly from under the bangs of her brown pageboy haircut, arm resting at her side. After a time, new characters of different personalities, even babies, were clipped to join the clans and populate my private world. Their escapades were endless, ranging far beyond Maple Street, Eaton, or even the state of Ohio. Full of romance, danger, and intrigue.

The gray hours would pass unnoticed until the swish of rain could be heard in the driveway to the garage, and the back screen door would slam with a bang announcing the arrival of Mother. The paper dolls would be packed in their boxes for another day. Wednesday afternoon was over.

Rena and Serafina could do whatever I imagined, whatever I could dream, whatever I hoped for or dared not do myself. They could fight, cry, love, or long for things in ways I could not. They could always win and have their way. They were counselors and friends, the sisters I never had, and my teachers in ways the generous lady from the fabric store never could have known. They taught me that as long as there is imagination and a Wednesday afternoon, I would never need to be lonely.

Time Capsule

On a warm but windy Thursday in late autumn, I found myself sharing a bag lunch with a small group of dusty people in the kitchen of a very old farmhouse on State Route 503 about two miles north of Lewisburg, one of the small villages that encircle Eaton like planets in the solar system known as Preble County, Ohio. The kitchen had long been unused. The sunlight from the recently unshuttered window to the south reflected brightly on the white surfaces of the midcentury appliances and the table around which we were all crowded. We were on break from several hours of rummaging through the lives of the former occupants, through drawers, pantries, closets, and rooms that, in essence, had been undisturbed for thirty years—some for many, many decades more.

Most of our disheveled group were, ordinarily, well-kempt proper ladies from the Preble County Historical Society, including my new acquaintance, Janet, with whom I exercise on Monday and Wednesday mornings, and who introduced me to the others. One of the two gentlemen, Todd Miller, appraises antiques and arranges auctions and sales. The other was Kenneth Garber, accountant, organist for a church in Cincinnati, and also, my mother's first cousin. Todd Miller was shaking his head in wonder. "I've rarely seen anything like this," he said. "It's like opening a time capsule."

I thought, "No kidding! And what if you were me?" For him and the ladies, this was a matter of local history; for Kenneth and me, it was a family matter.

This farm once belonged to my great-grandparents, Allen and Adaline Garber, and was the home where Kenneth's father, Virgil, my maternal grandmother, Nina, and three other children were reared. Allen Garber, with his stern beard and black garb, was descended from a long line of German Baptist Brethren (Dunkards). Adaline, however, was not. She and her children broke the link with the Brethren for our particular line of the family. I often wonder how my life would have been different had that not happened.

The legend of Allen Garber in our family was that he had traveled all the way to Germany to acquire his Holstein cattle, an incredibly progressive act for his time. My aunt Ruth (my mother's younger sister) likes to joke that he went there for "poontang" at the same time, since his first wife had just died. She laughs hysterically at the idea, as though it were utterly preposterous. I have always thought, "Maybe it isn't."

The farm on State Route 503 was eventually owned by my grandmother's sisters Vina and Alpha. To me, growing up, those names had a quaint, peculiar ring, as did their appearance—poorly groomed, raw boned, and clothed in shapeless dresses and aprons, breasts drooping toward their waists. Alpha, true to her name, was tall and dominant, long graying locks of hair loosely pulled back into a bun; whereas Vina was short and obsequious with a haircut apparently achieved by placing a bowl over her head. Alpha was a spinster, but Vina had married a chemist (Uncle Ike) who left his profession to farm the property.

From left: Vina, Kenneth, Grandma Nina, Arleene, me as a baby, and Alpha at the Garber farm circa 1940.

After their deaths, the farm fell into the hands of Arleene, the daughter of Ike and Vina who had modeled her life, apparently, on Aunt Alpha and never married. Arleene left the property to Kenneth. Now he had donated the land and the house and all its contents to Preble County. Members of the Preble County Historical Society were there to separate the contents of the house into three categories: articles to be displayed in a number of rooms intended to be restored and opened to the public, articles to be sold by Kenneth at auction, and articles to be discarded (i.e., trash). I had come to help and, incidentally, to look, touch, and listen for clues to my own genetic and ancestral past.

When my mother, Helyn, stumbled away from her failed marriage, she came home to Eaton with me, age three, in tow. We moved in with Grandma Nina, recently widowed and still living at 824 North Maple Street. Between my mother and Grandma Nina was a considerable generation gap, which created some tension to which I was not entirely oblivious. Actually, it was pretty funny.

My mother was a college-educated modern woman of the forties who earned her living as an English and physical-education teacher. She loved poetry and movement, especially acrobatic dancing, at which she was exceptionally gifted. Nina, like her sisters, was a grade-school-educated countrywoman, spoiled as a girl, with a tendency to whine and complain. She was gruff in manner, stubborn, and closed-minded to the point of bigotry. "Why couldn't you marry an American, like your father and grandfather?" she would say to me, years later, when I ran off with a Jewish boy from New York. Nina irritated and embarrassed my mother to the point of total exasperation, so much so that by the time I was twelve, we had moved to an apartment on Main Street above a podiatrist's office.

But Nina didn't suffer half the ridicule my mother and her two sisters directed at the aunts on the old farm north of Lewisburg which had neither running water nor electricity until the seventies. At least my mother and her sisters saw to it that Nina, unlike Alpha and Vina, wore corsets, stockings, and decent shoes. That her graying red hair was neatly braided and piled on top of her head. And most of all, that she didn't carry buckets and rags and save newspapers, clothing, and junk until it was lined up along every wall and stuffed into every possible closet and piece of furniture. Such habits, in our family, defined a Garber Girl, especially the never-throwing-anything-away part of it, which is

The Place Just Right

still a joke among the girl cousins, even today, in my generation. Therefore, Mr. Todd Miller, appraiser and member of the board of the Preble County Historical Society, had no idea of the implications when he described this old farmhouse as a "time capsule," and furthermore, as a "treasure trove." It was a vindication for Alpha and Vina and Nina, the original Garber Girls, and an unconscious slap at my mother and her thoroughly modern sisters, a joke that, unfortunately, only Kenneth, Aunt Ruth, and I are left to enjoy.

It is rare and enlightening for me, in my maturity, to walk across the land and through the rooms where my great-grandparents lived and labored. A wonderful twist of fate to find them much as they were not only when I was a girl, but when my grandmother was young as well. To see again the enormous dark wood wardrobes, bedsteads, hutches and chests, the handmade chairs and tables I barely noticed on visits as a child. To discover in trunks and drawers wonderful old garments from every decade of this past century and a few before, garments amazing in their richness and design, telling me that as girls, the drooping old ladies I knew were actually quite stylish and elegant. To find quilts and pieces of quilts and needlework attesting to their skill at sewing. To handle dishes and utensils in the kitchen and old pantry that must have been handled over and over by Adaline, Alpha, and Vina, day after day, year after year. And to realize from the excited looks in the eyes of the women and men with me that after all their use and mundane living, these objects retain a value never dreamed of by Adaline and her daughters. They will actually be on display for visitors to wonder who those people were who used them so long ago. Already that windy Thursday, the ladies from the Historical Society were talking about Adaline, Alpha, and Vina as though they actually knew them. A familiarity born, I suppose, of being so close to the things that were theirs.

Kenneth was gracious enough to invite Aunt Ruth and me to accompany him to the farmhouse, without the Historical Society and before the auction, to help sort through the final chest of unsorted personal items, and to select some small thing as a keepsake. Among hundreds of church bulletins and what seemed like thousands of inspirational newspaper clippings, apparently kept by Arleene, Ruth discovered a clipping of her wedding announcement from the forties complete with a picture of her I had never seen. I found a letter that I had written to Alpha and Vina from Italy when I was there on a college study tour in 1960, proving, at least for me, that I had been important enough in their lives that a trace of me remained along with so much else.

As for the keepsake, Ruthie chose a plate she recognized from many meals eaten there when she was a child. I went directly to something I had discovered in a bureau drawer the first day I had gone there to help. She has a china head with molded yellow curls, blue eyes, and painted rosy cheeks. Her tightly stuffed cloth body is dressed in an ancient white linen undergarment with lace tatting around legs covered in blue cotton stockings. She wears a beige linen dress with a checked border and sports a blue silk cape. I'm not sure whose doll she was—perhaps my grandmother's—it is now impossible to know. But when I hold her and cuddle her next to me, as I will on occasion, I do know I am holding a part of my own distant past next to my heart. I am only now learning how precious that is.

The Alpha Garden Club: Barriers

The spirit of my mother still dances in this town like a wisp of smoke caught in a late autumn breeze. It's my fault. I brought her here to her final resting place. I should have remembered she had been a very restless woman. It wouldn't be any different now.

"Baumhart," Kate Brown repeated at the Alpha Garden Club when I told her my last name, hoping for some sign of recognition. "The only Baumhart I knew was Helyn."

"That was my mother," I answered.

"Then you must be Brenda," she said, and smiled. "Oh my! I remember you when you were only so high," she said, putting her palm to the floor about three feet up. "Your mother was such an interesting girl." And after we had chatted a bit about the connection, how close she had been to Mother's best friend, she confided, "We felt so bad for your mother. She had a terrible time during that divorce. The family were politicians, weren't they?"

I nodded yes, but I wasn't looking at her anymore. I was looking through a window into the past at yet another image of my mother. This one was a rare glimpse, a vision of her very young, vulnerable and in terrible pain.

I thought about young Helyn all through the lunch of chicken, rice, and cranberry-walnut gelatin, saw her face among the flowers in the famous gardens featured in the slide show, and when I got home, I brought out the black notebook of her collected poetry. After some searching through the aging onionskin pages, I found what I was looking for:

BARRIER

Through many nights I've lain
And heard your quiet breath,
And wept to know a wall,
Less scalable than death.

I wonder if my mother, when she meticulously collected, typed, and made carbon copies of the poetry she had written into that black notebook, ever hoped, thought, knew, it would be a link between us. A legacy. An inheritance. A heart-to-heart talk through the years. The kind of heart-to-heart talk we never had in person. It's impossible now to know and probably presumptuous of me to imagine I was in her thoughts at all. After all, in those tender days I was only "so high," and she must have been preoccupied with her own need to make sense of her life and feelings. I can relate to that.

This, however, I do know. I was very much in her thoughts in the fall of 1961 when, after completing college, I moved back home to Eaton for the last time until now. In those days she paid close attention to my every move—as I got up each morning and drove along the Eaton Lewisburg Road to the little village school where I was teaching, and as I went out every night with the boy she hated and feared more than any boy I had ever brought home before. I couldn't understand it. Her behavior was absolutely inexplicable. She was at her wit's end.

To him she was rude, distant, a constant embarrassment. To me she was accusatory, irrational and interfering, impossible to live with. If I sat with him in the car late at night, she would come to the car window and bang on it for me to come in. If he and I were laughing or flirting in the house, she would slam doors and remind me how late it was getting to be. It was unbearable; I heard nothing she had to say. She was too provincial to be credible, undoubtedly menopausal, certainly small-minded and prudish. I absolutely couldn't tolerate it a moment longer.

The Place Just Right

"So high"—me with Mama.

Later, after the boy and I had eloped one October weekend and were married in a barbershop in North Carolina because the barber was also the justice of the peace, she shut me out. When I came to get my things, she snubbed me. When I called, she was barely interested. She never visited. I was hurt to the core. So, apparently, was she.

It was a chasm between us that never quite closed, an unspoken memory that never got the airing it sorely needed—an explanation, an apology that never came from either one of us. How I wish just once before she died my mother had said, "I'm sorry I abandoned you. I couldn't live it all again. It was just too painful."

I looked down at the black notebook, now cracked and fraying at the corners, reread the poem she wrote when she was so young and vulnerable, and whispered to my mother's spirit, still dancing in this town, "You were right about that boy. I'm so sorry I couldn't hear you."

Eaton High School, Class of 1957

Memories are long in a small town, and people, for the most part, have generous hearts.

I had thought, after more than forty years, I would return to Eaton, Ohio, as a stranger. However, I have found a welcome after all thanks to the warmth of my elderly aunt and uncles, good-hearted women's groups, and the persistence of Judy Timms Hacker, the keeper of the Eaton High School class of 1957, and the self-designated mother of us all.

Before I had moved back to Eaton, on a house-hunting visit, I called Judy (who, in the years she knew my address, had faithfully sent news of classmates and of reunions) to ask if we could lunch. I intended to learn what it was like now to live in Eaton. She surprised me at the Country Kitchen at the truck stop with twenty classmates. It was a chaos of laughs and screams as I gazed into faces after forty years desperately trying to associate this old lady or that with the girls I only vaguely remembered, while Judy, carrot-topped still, stood aside smiling devilishly all the while. I think she lives for such encounters.

I had been in Eaton only a few months when Judy gathered the next meeting of the ladies of the class of 1957, again about twenty women; however, not all of them the same ones who greeted me earlier. We assembled at the lodge by Lake Lakengren around a long table, autumn colors sparkling through the large windows, a tray of cold meat, bread, and cheese to the side, and shared our lives since graduation. We were instantly comfortable with each other as though it had been only yesterday we sat together in the school cafeteria, clustered in the halls wearing bobby socks and poodle skirts with crinolines, or argued about communism and the A-bomb in Mr. Williams's social studies classes. Nobody held back.

We heard the quiet accumulation of the ups and downs of forty years of living: years that traveled through the conformity of the fifties, the rebellions of the sixties, all the way to the new millennium, set against the uniquely shared knowledge of where we had all begun. One starting point of innocence and hope. Twenty different paths taken. As everyone took her turn recapping her life, a tone of confession, of release, slowly crept in. Rosalie had lost a child; Janet had raised one with cerebral palsy, was still caring for him at home. One had cancer; another had lost her husband recently, was struggling to live life alone. Another was divorced.

Some women happily described simple lives spent on the farm surrounded by children and grandchildren. Others told of success, businesses thriving, hard work rewarded. There was humor and laughter. Courage and confusion. There were disjointed lives, frenetic and incomplete. But the climax came when one classmate, encouraged by Judy, began to share the recent death of her youngest boy from AIDS. All of us, without embarrassment, cried with her as she described the return of her worldly young son to helpless infancy and to the care of the mother who had given him life in the first place. It was a moment of surprising closeness that made us all eager to meet again soon.

However, the third meeting of the ladies, held almost a year later, was a scene from a different play. Again there were twenty or so women; again the cast changed slightly, and the tone turned raucous and funny as we all began to recall the embarrassments and humiliations of being teenage girls. First periods, first kisses, crushes and heartbreaks. But the headline act of this show was the return of the prodigal, Betty Jane, the most popular and envied girl in the class of 1957 and clearly this year's project for Judy Timms Hacker.

To understand the appeal of Betty Jane, it is necessary to remember the fifties. Picture a scene from *Happy Days*, a drive-in where burgers and milkshakes are served on trays hooked to the car window as '55 Fords and Chevy pickup trucks cruise, cocky young men in ducktail haircuts whistling and yelling out the windows. We had such a drive-in, as well as a soda shop on Main Street with deep booths (jukeboxes at the back) for giggling and sharing gossip.

Remember also *The Last Picture Show*, in which restless small-town adolescents experiment with sex in the backseats of cars, spoiled beauty queens break the hearts of local sports heroes, and everyone knows if you don't eventually leave on the dusty bus that rolls into town once a week, you will be destined to slog through the same lousy, excruciatingly dull lives your parents lived. We had such a bus. And when it came to pick up Robert Carico and Bruce Hickey for basic training shortly after graduation, Linda Kay Walker and Jane Coffman, who were not their sweethearts, only friends, accompanied them to the bus stop and passionately kissed them goodbye to impress recruits picked up in other small towns who were now staring enviously out the window.

Now know that Betty Jane was the baton-twirling champion of the entire state of Ohio. In a small town in the fifties where high-school sports and their female complements of cheerleading and baton twirling were a galvanizing preoccupation, this was major celebrity, and Betty Jane was truly the best. She often performed publicly at sports events and civic gatherings, and those performances were always thrilling. Like a juggler, she kept the silver whirling object in constant motion—first with one hand, then passed back and forth with both hands. She twirled it over her head; she twirled it while somersaulting and sometimes while posing like a ballerina in arabesque.

But the most spectacular parts of her routine were the tosses. With a quick flick of the wrist, the baton would be off in the sky, sometimes one baton, sometimes two, even three. A couple of turns, a glance upward, and they would be caught—behind the back, through the legs, still whirling, no visible pause. On very important occasions there would be special sticks set afire shooting sparks into the twilight sky as Betty Jane kept them spinning. Oh, how the girls envied her. Even at the reunion, all these years later, how they went on about it. She captured for all of us a certain feminine perfection of the times—vivacity, skill, grace, and personality on display in her fringed satin shorts and tasseled boots. The American Spirit full of energy and heart; fresh faced and innocent, twirling and spinning with youth, determination, and an excess of joy. Contagious.

Even I was captured for a time—me, the incipient cynic. I wanted desperately to be a majorette, went to tryouts in great anticipation. Only the band director wouldn't let me do it. "You can read music," he said, almost accusingly. "I'm not going to waste you on that." So while the rest of the girls strutted up front and showed off their legs on chilly autumn football nights, I trudged around in the marching band in ill-fitting ugly gold pants and a purple jacket, wearing a hat that kept falling over my eyes, pinging on the glockenspiel, feeling clunky and deprived.

And did Betty Jane on her return to the class of 1957 remember her triumphs with gratitude and fondness? For those who have grown up to see what happened to the fifties, the answer is preordained. "I hated it," she said. "I couldn't stand it. I just wanted to be normal and not have to go to all those competitions and miss out on everything."

This to choruses of "Oh, really?" and "You don't mean it!" from the group. When I thought about it, I remembered I had known that. Her mother had been the Ohio equivalent of Rose from *Gypsy*, stage mother of baton twirling, fulfilling her own dreams through her daughter. After all, Betty Jane and I had been friends, even though she was on the first tier of popularity, and I considered myself to be on the second, just below Betty Jane, Jane Coffman, and Linda Kay Walker. Ask any female teenager back then, or even now for that matter, and she could have told you pretty specifically where she stood in the pecking order in high school. Such things become imprinted for life.

The story is, in fact, even sadder than that. Betty Jane married the boy of her dreams, a sports hero, of course, before they even finished high school. The baby came soon after. Over the years I heard snippets of information about her life. He became a minister; there were five more children; they lived in several places. And then, suddenly, she was back in Eaton alone. Several years ago, Mr. Sports Hero/Christian minister divorced her amid rumors of his involvement with a woman from the church. "I'm so embarrassed," she told me, tears in her eyes and obviously still devastated. "I still love him, always will. There is a huge empty place in my heart."

The dreams of girls in the fifties were simple: popularity, romance, and enduring love. All the things we saw in the movies. They were uncomplicated dreams totally incompatible with reality. Some of us found that out early. Others found it out late. But in one way or another, the girls of the class of 1957 became women.

Judy Timms Hacker made damn sure Betty Jane got to that gathering, even if it did take ten phone calls. I plan to call her soon myself. Maybe I can get her out to lunch.

My Father's World

In the convention-ridden forties and fifties, especially in the provincial Midwest, divorce was not the commonplace proposition it is today. Back then, I believed I was the only girl alive who lived in two worlds: my mother's (workaday Eaton), and my father's (my own magical kingdom called Vermilion).

Vermilion, Ohio, hugs the shore of Lake Erie about 225 miles north and east of Eaton. In those years it was a village of about three thousand people, smaller than Eaton at about five thousand folks, but infinitely more fascinating. Several times during the school year, I would be put on a train in Dayton and met by my father or grandfather in nearby Wellington. However, during summer vacations, my mother brought me to Vermilion herself and rented a place for the season so I could spend time with my grandparents, whom both she and I adored.

Vermilion was divided into north and south by Routes 2 and 6 coming out of Cleveland to Sandusky. Both places were enticing: Cleveland, with its dirty, busy ports and tall buildings; and Sandusky, where we could visit the Cedar Point amusement park or take a ferry or a rickety old Ford tri-plane to Put-in-Bay, a delightful island in Lake Erie boasting caves, wineries, and a monument to Oliver Perry and his famous sea victory over the British in the War of 1812. Eaton had no ports, no caves, no ferries, and, certainly, no wineries.

Vermilion itself was made up of worlds within worlds to be discovered and savored. Along the shore on the eastern edge of the village were four such worlds, right in a row, like a series of sets on the lot of a movie studio. The farthest east of these was Crystal Beach, a second-rate amusement park with a huge dance hall where the big bands of the forties played. Nokomis Park came next, separated only by a fence easily scaled by someone who wanted to enter Crystal Beach for free. Nokomis was a modest resort consisting of several long blocks of summer cabins leading to a frightening wooden staircase steeply descending to the beach.

Linwood Park followed, a much larger resort of summer homes where the cabins all sported huge screened-in front porches and sat on mysterious, heavily shaded streets strewn with pine needles. Finally, between Linwood Park and the Vermilion River, the Lagoons sprawled with ostentatious pride. This particular neighborhood almost lived up to its pretentious name. There actually were a few lagoons branching off the river. It was very exclusive. I wasn't invited in often. Waterfront property, it was designed to be seen from a boat on the river. A view from the road offered only garages and backyards.

The playful girl who was then my mother and I lived for several summers in what we laughingly referred to as "the Shack" in Nokomis, a two-room, haphazard cabin with cots for beds. My best friend, Molly, lived in a summerhouse on the most desirable lot in the place, the last one on the street to the lake at the top of a steep staircase to the beach. This was a true summer home with knotty-pine-paneled walls, a great room, a fireplace, and a second story of unfinished but comfortable bedrooms in which Molly and I, like true best friends, would giggle, gossip, and dream together from our cots long past bedtime. Often we could hear music from the dance hall. I had friends in Eaton, but with no one did I feel as free as I did with Molly. We were perpetually on vacation—spent the entire day on the beach, no schoolyard intrigues or pecking orders, just girls having fun.

When I was in my early teens, Mother and I found yet another set on which to do our summer play, shabby Acorn Lodge in the woods along the Vermilion River, accessible only by the most terrifying roller-coaster road I have ever driven. I still drive that road in my nightmares. Acorn Lodge rented for three hundred dollars a summer. It was one room and a bath the size of a stall in a gas-station restroom. The shower was outdoors. In the living area—a space with bare wooden walls—three bunk beds were lined up along one wall and an enormous table was placed under a barely shaded lightbulb hanging from a cord to the ceiling. Two more cots rested damply behind the screens of the porch, where I loved to sleep on stormy nights.

Acorn Lodge was one of several cut-rate vacation cabins carelessly built in the river bottom and usually rented to vacationers by the week. On the weekends

The Place Just Right

Cottage - Vermilion River Park - 1952

we were treated to raucous parties from adjoining cabins. Nevertheless, we loved it. Steamy summer nights, we would gather with friends and play sextuple or more solitaire, leaping across the big table to slam cards on somebody else's piles, laughing until we were out of breath. Once or twice during the summer, we would rent a canoe, put it in the Vermilion River a few hundred yards from our door, and spend the day exploring, often as far as the shale banks several miles upstream, where we would have our picnic.

For a precious few summers we lived an idyllic life in Vermilion, Ohio, and I remember it just that way—carefree, flawless, joyful, and full of laughter and comradeship. Whatever God gave me those summers gave me a vision for the rest of my life. From those summers I learned to live with the expectation of happiness—knowing positively how much delight can come from such simple things. I was a somewhat lonely and withdrawn child of divorce. Those summers carried me through many long, gray winters in Eaton, Ohio. As an adult, the memory of those good times still carry me through many other dreary times.

Angel Flight: An After-Christmas Story

These are the days following Christmas, and the morning television newscast is full of advice on how to avoid post-holiday letdown. Too late for me. From beyond the frozen furrows of the empty cornfields dusted with yesterday's light snow, down the mostly deserted streets of my neighborhood, past the few remaining lightbulb reindeer eerily bobbing their electric heads in the wind, my Christmas memories have come calling. Like Scrooge, I take the hand of the Ghost of Christmas Past and wander through time, peering at the tender scenes and familiar faces now forever gone, overcome with that peculiarly Victorian sadness that is the heart and soul of melodrama. It is a pathos too sweet and cloying for the serious business of daily living, but hard to avoid in the quiet lassitude of these short, gray Ohio days following Christmas.

It always seemed to me the winter snow that fell in Vermilion, where I spent most Christmases at the home of my grandparents, was an entirely different sort than that which whistled down on the barren fields in Eaton. Filled with the moisture of the ever-dominant Lake Erie, it was heavier, softer, cozier, like a fat, spongy pillow, as lickable as white cotton candy. It piled up around the house, insulating it against the cold, making it appear like a cottage in some fanciful cloud kingdom.

At 824 North Maple Street in Eaton, snow made the house seem dark, cave-like—the heavy draperies drawn against drafts, people huddled under blankets or near the heat registers reluctant to move until the temperature rose. On Huron Street in Vermilion, snow brought brightness that sparkled through the glassed-in areas of the front and back porches and into the little room to the west with the black-and-white-checkered tile floor, the fern, and the noisy parakeet

The Place Just Right

Grandmother Frances

called Boy Blue. That room was referred to, even in winter, as the sunroom. My grandparents' house on Huron Street was neither bigger nor richer than 824. However, Huron Street was prettier, with Oriental carpet, colorful, overstuffed couches and chairs, and a magnificent fireplace, and was filled with the infectious laughter of my step-grandmother, Frances.

In the forties and early fifties, television was not yet a part of our lives, so evenings on Huron Street were spent quietly. I still remember with joy long Monopoly marathons and staying up late struggling to complete a huge jigsaw puzzle before the holidays ended. Often we would pop popcorn in a special mesh basket over the flames at the fireplace.

One Christmas Eve, when I was still a tiny little girl, I noticed some of the kernels of popcorn were dark red instead of the usual yellow and asked Frances why that was. She told me the red kernels were magic, and if I wrapped one in a wee felt bag, which she produced, and put it in the Christmas tree, something wonderful would happen on Christmas morning. I eagerly tucked a red kernel into the little bag, found a spot for it among the branches, and went to bed waiting not only for Santa, but also for something else wonderful besides.

In the morning a magnificent angel adorned the top of the Christmas tree. Her robe was red tissue paper, her face and hair were those of a beautiful lady, and her wings spreading wide behind her were lined with tinsel. When I look at her now (and I still have her, carefully wrapped in a box of Christmas ornaments), I can see how she was lovingly made from what was at hand in the house. But on that Christmas long ago, as I looked up at her out of reach high on the tree, she was the most beautiful angel I could have ever imagined. I brought all the children from the neighborhood to see her and to hear the story of how she came to be there. She was to give us blessings through the holidays, Frances explained, and when we took down the tree, she would fly back to where she had come from—heaven, we presumed, or fairyland.

That year, as always, the long cinnamon-scented days turned slowly, but inevitably, toward the New Year, and soon it was time to take down the tree. We assembled the ornament boxes neatly on the couch in preparation. As we began, sadly, to remove the tinsel, the doorbell rang and was opened to a small crowd of children: scrawny Nancy Lee from next door to the east; the Maynard kids, tall, slouchy Jeanette and shy Warren; ragamuffin Pat Keller from across the street; and three or four Williams kids, including their cousin, Bobby, red hair and freckles standing out boldly in the winter sun. They were there, they said skeptically, "...to watch the angel fly away to heaven." I like to think had I been even one year older, I might have thought to look at my grandmother Frances and see her turn a little pale. But I was still a tiny little girl, and I, too, wanted to see the flight of the angel.

We were not disappointed that day. It wasn't too far into the removal of the tinsel, not long after the cookies and milk and the recitations of who got what for Christmas, when came a mysterious rustling of wings, a flash of red color somewhere near the top of the tree, and she was gone—the angel had flown. Nobody quite saw her leave the room—she certainly didn't go out the door; several of the children ran outside to see. Perhaps, we thought, she was capable of going through the glass of the windows. Or even up the chimney. But she was definitely gone. We had heard it—we even thought we saw it. The miracle of angel flight. And there on the floor, conspicuous among the light cords and discarded tinsel—a single red kernel of corn.

It became a tradition, an important part of Christmas on Huron Street in Vermilion, Ohio. Incredibly, each year there was an additional angel until there were six or seven on the Christmas tree and six or seven flights. And every year, try though we might, we never figured it out. It was always the same—a rustle of wings, a flash of color, a kernel of corn, and the tinkling laughter of Grandmother Frances.

When teaching high school a few years ago, I was touched to discover that many of my female students believed in angels. They liked to write about them in their essays, draw pictures of them, and, I suppose, talk to them in the quiet of their darkened rooms at night. Most of their angels had names, especially the guardian angels. I taught in a poor, immigrant neighborhood where families struggled to put food on the table, and daily life was often mean and violent. Angels were very important to young girls in such surroundings. I respected that. Moreover, I understood it from deep within my being. My life as a child was neither mean nor violent, but it was confusing, sometimes sad, often bleak and lonely. Still, I was luckier than my students were. Not only did I have a guardian angel, she was incarnate as well in the person of Grandmother Frances.

I cannot say if Frances came from heaven or merely from Cadiz, Ohio, as she claimed. When I was a child, they could have been one and the same place—since I didn't remember having been to either. But it is easy to believe that wherever she came from, some place of unborn souls, she had been sent ahead to be my grandmother, instructed to cushion my rocky passage through childhood and to fly back as soon as that was accomplished. I know, even now, she is close enough to be watching over me. I feel her presence in the hot tears that decades later still roll from the corners of my eyes whenever I think of her. And once, shortly after she died, when I had spent a night of grief in a strange place at a new job far away from everyone I knew, I woke to feel the strong pressure of her arms around me as though she had held me tight throughout the long, torturing darkness.

A few days before Christmas this year, I had an email message from Bobby Williams, the one person from Vermilion with whom I am again in touch. The message was short. "Merry Christmas. By the way, how did your grandmother make those angels disappear? Huck."

My message was equally brief. "Happy New Year. They flew back all by themselves. Didn't you know? Brenda."

Uncle Daisy

Weltha Norris, of all people, told me the news. From across Maple Street, Weltha watched me and my cousins grow up. She still keeps constant surveillance, apparently, because she always appears at the front door whenever I go to 824 to check on something for Ben, now a resident of Greenbriar Nursing Center. "Say," she said, her intense blue eyes suddenly bright. "Wasn't that your uncle in the Columbus paper? The one who just died?"

"That's the first I've heard of it," I answered, trying not to be irritated. You would have thought somebody could have notified me.

A few days later, somebody did. The Lorain National Bank sent me official notice in a stilted letter, intimating that since Mr. A. D. Baumhart, Jr., was deceased, I should expect certain legal matters regarding our joint inheritance (a trust from my grandmother Frances) to come under review. I immediately panicked. I felt certain nobody could take away my stipend from the trust, but this was Uncle Daisy (Dave). Paranoia with regard to any of his suspicious activities was part of my conditioning from childhood. Who knows what nefarious scheme he had put into motion, given his interminable dotage—even, perhaps, from beyond the grave?

Uncle Dave was my father's older brother, and he took up more space in a room than anyone had a right to do. It was not that he was so big—but that he was so dominating. Partly he commanded attention by his erect posture and immaculate dress, partly because of his imposing black hair and mustache, but mostly it was because of "the voice." He, like my grandfather and father, was blessed with an exceptionally resonant baritone voice that years of public speaking had trained into an instrument of almost Stradivarian variety. Coupled with his devilish charm and the repertoire of down-home anecdotes he had inherited from my grandfather, his voice made him the irresistible focus of constant attention.

It didn't hurt that he was a member of the United States House of Representatives and perceived by the locals to be an influential power broker. One of my earliest memories is of walking with him down Main Street in Vermilion, stopping every few steps for another adoring citizen to tip his hat, to bow and scrape, to curry favor, to touch his sleeve. I think he liked me back then. I rode in a red wagon with balloons when he ran for office. I still have pictures of him, resplendent in his naval officer's uniform, helping me raise the flag in our backyard, or holding me on his knee as with my plump baby fingers, I cautiously felt his thick mustache. In those days I knew him as Uncle Daisy.

My mother found him unbearable. She used to rattle him by knocking on the bathroom door when he was bathing, calling out, "Dave, I'm coming in!" Then she would open the door and send me in instead, barely walking and delighted into squeals at the spectacle of violently splashing water and towels flailing as he bolted out of the tub and grabbed for something to preserve his modesty. He was the perfect victim for such a joke. Pomposity was his middle name.

Throughout my childhood, he was hard to ignore—the most audible of the trio of males with rumbling voices that gathered in my grandparents' living room after Sunday dinner passing the box of White Owl cigars. I was transfixed because in my mother's house in Eaton, no robust male laughter echoed from the living room, no discussion of important affairs of state nor trails of cigar smoke drifted into the kitchen, where the women were scurrying to clean up. When Dave was present, everybody catered to his tastes, especially my step-grandmother, Frances, who must have felt acutely in his presence the fact that she was not his real mother, only a substitute tolerated for the sake of A.D., Sr.

Dave mostly ignored me after he got married. He did, however, extend himself when I went to the nation's capital my senior year in high school with a group of students hosted by the *Dayton Daily News*. He was omnipresent at every photo opportunity impressing everyone, especially the representatives of the newspaper, with his knowledge and reputation. I have a newspaper photo of him and me shaking hands on the steps of the Capitol, looking for all the world as if we were close—Uncle Daisy and niece sharing a moment in the spotlight.

The truth was, of course, we were not close unless it suited him, and that was rare. That did not save me from being witness, nevertheless, to some of the most revealing moments of his life, an exposure, upon reflection, I might have been better off without. Like the salesman who exists on "a smile and a shoeshine," like a balloon that bobs and impresses until stuck by a pin, Uncle Daisy turned out to be cheap veneer pasted over empty space, a robot programmed as a stereotypical politician that eventually short-circuits and becomes stuck, repeating its clichés over and over again.

The first time I saw the chink in Uncle Daisy's mask was the night my grandfather died. Albert David, Sr., at eighty-eight, suffered a stroke and was confined to a hospital bed set up in the former dining room on Huron Street, unable to speak coherently or to take care of himself in any way. He remained in that condition for nearly a year, cared for at home by occasional nurses, but mostly by Grandmother Frances, who barely left his side, waiting and praying for a "moment of lucidity" when she might say goodbye. She fervently did not want him to go before she had a chance to communicate those intimate things that only two people who had shared a life of love and dedication might want to say at its end. That moment had come and gone, and it was obvious to all of us in the room (Frances, the night nurse, the distraught doctor who was also his close friend, and me) that the end was near. We each did what we could, but mostly we waited, listening to his breathing become more labored and difficult as the long hours passed.

Shortly before midnight, Uncle Daisy burst into the room, overcoat flying open, slamming the door as he arrived. He surveyed the scene and demanded to know of the doctor, who by this time was hunched against a wall with his head in his hands, just what was being done. "Dave," the doctor said wearily, "we have done all we can. Your father is dying." Dave took one step toward the bed, took one look at his father's gray face and open mouth, paled, and bolted for the door. He was not seen again until hours after Grandfather finally wheezed his last breath, after the gentle moments of quiet tears and affectionate whispered goodbyes, after the undertaker had come and gone and Frances had silently climbed the stairs to creep alone into her marriage bed and sink into an exhausted sleep.

What I didn't realize until years later was that, by this time, Uncle Daisy had begun a long slide downward, a descending spiral including a divorce, the loss of his office as United States congressman, the squandering of much of my grandfather's estate, and a nearly three-year alcoholic binge that included my father's bailing him out of unpaid-for hotel rooms all over the upper Midwest. When I saw Uncle Daisy again, he was reduced to the most desperate of circumstances—constantly drunk, wearing stained trousers, and sleeping in an old car parked in the back lot of my grandfather's drugstore in downtown Vermilion. He had reached, as they say, rock bottom.

Charley

My mother and Grandmother Frances both believed drunkenness ran in families, most particularly in the Baumhart family. "There is a look," Mother would say. "All the drunks in the family have the same physical features—the same nose, facial mask." That was true even of the women, they thought. True of Cousin Bessie, who would often call Frances in the wee hours of the morning, drunk and rambling; also true of Cousin Susie, who, after a wild few decades, was now sober but still incorrigible.

It didn't help, thought my mother, that Vermilion was historically a fishing village. Men who were out on the lake all summer had nothing to do except sit in the warmth of convivial bars during the long winter when the lake was frozen over. Drinking in Vermilion was not the sin it was presumed to be in temperate, straitlaced Eaton. And then there was the war. Frances offered the opinion that some men who returned from World War II were never the same, couldn't quite get things together.

I grew up hearing these things discussed, sometimes in my presence, more often when they thought I was out of hearing. These were searching discussions, serious and sad in spite of their kitchen-table setting. They were seminars in coping, an early form of group therapy, attempts by two women married into the family to find some sort of conceivable excuse for their pain—to somehow explain the waste my father's life had become. Mother had washed her hands of him in hurt and disgust. Frances still clung to the hope he might yet turn his life around. Miracles had happened before.

My father, Charley, sometimes called Chubb or Bud, was four years younger than his brother, Dave, softer and more approachable. He had the easygoing charm and recklessness often associated with a second son forced to live in the shadow of an overachieving older brother. Charley had been an alcoholic most of his life, unlike Dave, whose drinking seemed to develop over the years. In college and during the time Charley had worked for the state government in Columbus, he developed a reputation as a wild partier and womanizer. He had, however, returned from his service in the navy and World War II to a plodding life in Vermilion. For a while he had been employed as an accountant with a trucking firm in Lorain, Ohio, but eventually gave that up in order to help out in the drugstore with his father. He would come home for lunch and a long nap every day and spend his evenings in a bar. He was functioning, after a fashion.

My father, Charley, and me circa 1960.

The Place Just Right

For a few years Charley did even better than that. He married again, albeit briefly, to a local woman, and was elected mayor of Vermilion, although it was always hinted that he won the election only because of his brother's reputation as congressman. Still, he loved being mayor, however it happened, amazed more than anyone by the incongruity. He walked through his mayoral functions like a naughty kid who, miraculously, had gotten away with a delightful impersonation. I will always remember him one Fourth of July, winking and grinning at me as the high-school band, a corps of majorettes, a fife and drum corps, several floats, horses and riders, and staid gentlemen in fezzes with tassels lined up on the corner of Huron and Division Streets awaiting his orders to proceed with the parade. Another time he came very close to laughing out loud, breaking character entirely, when he dragged me to Mayor's Court and tried to remain solemn throughout the hearing and adjudication of several heated local disputes.

Sadly, Charley was not mayor of Vermilion for long. By the time my grandfather died, he had moved out of his parent's house and into two rooms once used as a beauty parlor above the drugstore. He hadn't bothered to turn them into an apartment except to bring in a cot for sleeping. Several sinks were still lined up against the wall, and since he had no other furniture, he used them to hold his few belongings. He had inherited the store, but he was not a pharmacist, so he just kept the doors open for some time so he could sell off whatever merchandise remained. Later on, he rented the space to a gospel church, called himself the Man Upstairs, and threatened to one day open the door to his "apartment" and send down doves during the service.

About three years after Grandfather died, Uncle Dave returned to Vermilion from his long alcoholic odyssey through the Midwest, having finally reached the end of his money and his considerable influence. Frances's demeanor on the telephone had alarmed me, so against her protestations, I came to see what was happening. I found her under siege, not only from my father and Dave, who wanted to borrow money, but from the town authorities as well. They were unhappy Dave was sleeping in an old car behind the drugstore on Main Street and wandering the streets during the day in filthy clothes. They wanted Frances to solve the deteriorating problem.

Frances was in poor health at the time, and I, in my early twenties, was in over my head, but between us we did our best to deal with the situation. We started with Charley, always the more malleable of the two, and for possibly the first time in his life, the more responsible. I was sent as an unlikely emissary to enlist his help in committing Dave to a state hospital. It was not clear whether either Frances, as stepmother, or I had the legal power to do it. Charley clearly did.

I found Charley at the bar across the street from the drugstore and broached the proposition. At first he wouldn't hear of it, but eventually, he came around. Maybe it was because I had never been involved in such family matters before. Possibly it was out of pity for Frances's plight, maybe out of concern for his brother, but he roused himself out of his haze and asked me to take him to the doctor for injections of B vitamins, believed then to be an aid to drying out. He had to get sober fast.

I can still recall how pale and out of condition his upper body looked as he sat in the doctor's office without his shirt. I don't think I had ever seen my father unclothed. We had rarely even been together in the same house for more than a few days since I was three years old. Yet, here we were, overseeing together a family crisis. It strengthened a bond that, until then, had been tenuous. It affirmed a relationship that had always been an enigma for both of us, a curiosity. I was grateful to him; I even admired him for digging down deep and finding the strength to cope, to take charge, however briefly.

Charley was insistent on one point, however. Before we drove to Sandusky, before we saw any judge, before Charley signed any papers, and before the "men in white suits" came to get Uncle Dave, he wanted to try to get Dave voluntarily to do it for himself. Charley said to me, "I want to give him his dignity." So we trundled over to the drugstore to meet with Uncle Daisy.

Baumhart's Drugstore

When I was growing up, my grandparents' drugstore was a child's paradise. Sweet treats crammed the candy case and fountain. New toys were constantly being unloaded from trucks in sturdy brown boxes. Hidden drawers held mysterious grown-up objects and potions. I remember the drugstore in many seasons and moods, but no mood more bizarre than the one I experienced that night my father, Charley, and I crossed Main Street to meet my drunken uncle Dave with the intention of persuading him to commit himself to the state hospital.

As we entered the darkened store, we seemed to be escorted by a yellow beam of light from the street that fell directly onto the dusty glass surface of the candy case now emptied of the licorice sticks and wax bottles of colored sugar water I had arranged so meticulously as a child. The candy case, in turn, redirected the light into the mirror behind the soda fountain, where it diffused into a glow and illuminated only that small section of the large rectangular room.

The soda fountain and stools, the mirror, stacked soda mugs, and taps for phosphate and soda water could easily have been mistaken for a bar in the weak light from the street. The dark wood of the nearly empty shelves and tables beyond created eerie shadows representing whatever the imagination could conceive—customers hunched together in conversation, high-backed booths hiding secret acts and words, chairs upturned on tables after hours. It was as if the soda fountain where so many children had come on summer days to sip lime phosphates and lick strawberry ice cream cones had been transformed into Harry Hope's saloon in O'Neill's *The Iceman Cometh*, where it was possible to drown one reality in a bottle and create another out of the reflections in a glass.

When Charley and I got there, Dave was nowhere to be seen, so he entertained me while we waited. He shared with his father and brother a great joy in telling a story. He began:

"I look at you, and I remember the day I saw you born.

'Charles,' your mother said. 'Charles, I think it might be advisable if we started for the hospital.'

I said, 'How long have you been in labor?'

'Eight hours,' she said. Jesus God, I got her out of there so fast I forgot her suitcase.

Then when we got there, the nurse said to me, 'You might as well go on home; it's still pretty early.' Christ, was your mother mad.

Now there's a woman who had a huge mole sitting right in her navel. I said to the doctor, 'Shouldn't that thing be removed?'

'It won't affect the delivery,' he said. Jesus, he must have been some kind of nut."

"Some kind of nut" was the punch line for most of Charley's stories, and it was always accompanied by the same wide-eyed, startled look of amazement at the follies of humankind so characteristic of his personality. A stool at a bar is a fabulous place to observe the foibles of human beings, as is a drugstore on Main Street in a small town. My grandfather broke into uncontrollable laughter, tears running down his face, every time he told the story of the man who came into the store each day to buy a dish of ice cream. The man would shovel the ice cream into his mouth as fast as he could as though it might melt if he didn't hurry. Then he would grab his head and moan as the cold ice cream, eaten too fast, produced the inevitable terrible headache. He never learned, and apparently, in all those years, nobody ever pointed out the simple reason he was in so much pain. It must have been far too entertaining to watch his stupidity.

Into this quiet, dimly lit scene, in the midst of these reflections on human folly, Uncle Daisy appeared, not quietly or humbly as one might suppose given his desperate circumstances, but suddenly and aggressively, with his usual commanding air. He was wearing an expensive silk suit, and although his inebriation was evident from frequent close calls with his balance, his manner was dignified and remarkably poised. The suit itself was rumpled and stained, yet he was wearing with it a neatly tied necktie.

Ignoring me, Dave came in as a man on a mission insisting Charley give his immediate attention to "a matter of great importance." I remember my father told him just as quickly he didn't have any money, if that was the matter in question, and to please take off his (Charley's) tie since it was the only decent one he owned. And with that, Dave left as abruptly as he had arrived, announcing with great condescension that he would attempt again to discuss his "matter of urgent necessity" in the morning when Charley might be more coherent. So much for that, I thought. So much for my father's notion of giving the man his dignity.

But it was not to be over so quickly. Shortly after he left, Dave returned looking confused. "Charles, I find I need the keys to your car. Where have you put them?" This time Charley was more hospitable and offered him a drink.

Dave relaxed enough to reveal that he "had a very important appointment in Cleveland at precisely ten o'clock in the morning, and since [he was] a little short of ready cash for the taxi fare, hoped that [Charley] would forward it." A bus was out of the question since the busses came so irregularly. When pressed, he confessed it was a job interview with a "very prestigious firm in an extremely responsible position."

At that point my father lost it, pointing out with great exasperation that, given the way Dave was behaving, he could hardly expect to be let into the restroom of the county bank, let alone into an interview at a reputable business.

For a minute it looked as though he had gotten through. Dave paused for a very long time as though he were deep in thought and confessed that he was very tired and, perhaps, needed a rest in order to regain his "health." That was the opening we had been waiting for, and within a few minutes, we had the night nurse for the state hospital on the phone. Then my father made his fatal mistake. He handed the phone to Dave.

In his most melodious tones, Dave introduced himself as the former congressman and asked the name of the nurse. We heard him thanking her for her support, accepting her gratitude for his having helped a neighbor's son who had gone to West Point, gossiping about the new representative. He did think to inquire about the admissions procedures for …hospital rest…for a dear friend about whom he was most concerned. Then we heard him say: "No, it's not really an emergency. I see, from nine in the morning? Well, thank you very much, my dear. You've been an enormous help. God bless you. Goodbye."

As he prepared to leave, my father asked, "You're not going to the hospital then?"

Dave replied, "Why, Charles, I don't see how that would be possible, do you? I have an appointment at ten in the morning. Good night."

By ten the next morning, my father and I were in Sandusky in the office of a judge. My father's hands shook as he signed the papers, but by the end of the day, Dave was committed for ninety days to the state hospital. We heard the sheriff found him in Rubberneck Park, and that he went quietly. After the required ninety days, Dave was, apparently, fully recovered. He remarried, and, I presume, spent the rest of his days in complete control of his faculties. I saw him only twice more—once at the reading of my grandmother's will, and for the final time, at my father's funeral.

Grandmother Frances was an exceptionally caring person, never known to be vindictive. But after these events, she took a subtle revenge through the instrument of her will. Instead of leaving us all of her money directly, she established a trust that paid to Dave, my father, and me the munificent sum of a hundred dollars per month, each. When this arrangement was read to the assembled heirs, Dave left the room with a nosebleed. I hope Frances was watching.

Although we were able over the years to triple the disbursement, the trust has continued to grow, so the bank is now revisiting the matter through the courts—illustrating what I have been learning ever since I moved back to Ohio. The past cannot be trusted to remain there. It can always come back to twist its way around my life. So I watch amazed and amused as lawyers and bank officials read the words my beloved grandmother had written on her behalf so many years ago, trying to determine what should be done now. Knowing nothing and caring nothing about her heart and the human foibles that got us all to this place. I like to think Charley is also watching, equally amused and amazed.

My father died in the early seventies a year before his sixtieth birthday. He was found in his sink-lined domicile above the former drugstore alone, having choked on his own vomit. The funeral was small, but respectful, and Uncle Dave was in rare form, amusing us all with many charming anecdotes before and after the service. Before I left town, however, I stopped into the bar across the street from the drugstore to touch base with a few of my dad's cronies. A woman, apparently a special friend of my father's judging from the tears in her eyes, took me aside and shared what they were saying in the bar.

The night my father died, he had fallen ill, she said, and someone had called Dave, who took him to the hospital emergency room. Then Dave brought him back to his "apartment" and left. But here was the funny thing. When Charley's friends became worried about him and sent someone to see where he might be, the place was locked. Charley never locked it.

I wasn't quite sure what to make of all this. It was, after all, barroom gossip tinged with the musty smell and amber tones of imaginations spurred into fantasy by whiskey and beer. I pondered it on occasion, then let it slip back into the surreal world where it belonged. The world I will always associate with my father—and with Uncle Daisy. A world as difficult to make sense of as the shadows cast by a yellow street light through the windows of an abandoned store.

Vermilion Redux

Some months after the death of my uncle Dave in 2001, I was summoned to Sandusky for a pretrial hearing regarding the trust fund from my grandmother's will. Since Sandusky is only minutes from Vermilion, I decided that while I was there, I would visit the town for the first time since my father's funeral in 1973. I thought, "By now I ought to be used to revisiting the past. I might as well open one more door." So with some trepidation, I headed north from Eaton. I had no one to call. If I still had family there, I had no idea who they were. This visit would be about discovering how time had changed Vermilion. Or so I thought.

Instead, my visit turned out to be what we used to call, back in the hallucinogenic seventies, a head trip. I might as well have left my body behind in practical, grounded Eaton. It was impossible to know what was real, what was memory, what was illusion, and what was imagination. Totally alone, emotionally confused and vulnerable, I floated from place to place like a wraith. I was not even sure if I was visible to the people around me; not even sure that if I reached out to touch them, my hand wouldn't go right through their image into empty space. Sometimes in life, even without the help of hallucinogens, it is easy to believe we are indeed "such stuff as dreams are made on."

In my child's mind, Vermilion had always been a kingdom of the imagination anyway, a warm vision to ponder on a cold day in January. An exotic play land of carnivals and street dances with the band pulled along on a wagon and the sidewalks littered with confetti. A veritable library of true and historical adventures: shipwrecks, battles and monuments, exploration and romance. Though its scenery could often be tawdry, like an ancient funhouse, or pretentious, with its

The Place Just Right

marinas, yachts, and white-suited local sailors, there was also a natural beauty along the banks of the river and in the orchards and marshes surrounding the town. Its history is rich and colorful; its people, the ones I knew at any rate, tolerant of eccentricity and full of life. I hoped it would seem so still.

As I drove north toward Erie County, my first surprise was Lake Erie itself. I have always been thrilled, as in Los Angeles, for instance, to round a bend in a road and suddenly see spread out before me a great expanse of water, like driving off the end of the world. But as I neared the end of my journey in Ohio, I was inexplicably seized with anxiety, as though the water represented a void capable of expanding inward and absorbing all in its path. I found myself scanning the horizon, looking for the first signs of water, feeling it was playing hide-and-seek with me—seeming to be there, then transforming into a cloud before my eyes.

In spite of my love of swimming and the beach, I had forgotten I had actually been, at times, terrified of that blue void. Once, I almost drowned and had to be rescued from the pier. Another time, I had crashed into a rocky cliff at Crystal Beach on my inner tube, the victim of some sudden late-August swells. I spent the day in a peculiar approach/avoidance of the water, shying from it as it seemed to lick the edge of the road along the shore, welcoming it as I sat on new benches at the beach at the end of Main Street wondering if the mermaid I had always imagined sunning herself there would appear on the table rock I remembered, but could only now locate by occasional swirls of white water near the pier several hundred feet from shore.

In Vermilion what I expected to be the same wasn't; what I had expected to change hadn't. Surely, I assumed, Main Street would have been renovated with new shops for the tourists. I imagined a scene something like Santa Monica or Palm Beach with awnings and outdoor tables, perhaps a coffee shop. When I drove east into town on old Routes 2 and 6 (no longer heavily traveled because of the interstate highway several miles south) my predictions seemed to be coming true. Several old houses along that route were transformed into antique or gift shops, freshly painted with new entrances and welcoming lights and signs.

However, as I turned onto what had been the principal business street, I saw that the facades of the buildings were dingy and worn. In the middle of the day, it was deserted. The Baumhart's Drugstore building, our family name visible just below the roof, was still the shabby storefront gospel church it had been when my father lived on the second story among the sinks of the old beauty parlor. I didn't linger there, fearful of seeing the ghost of my grandfather, dressed in his three-piece suit, pocket watch in hand, just inside the entrance. Or the shape of my father shuffling toward the bar across the street. It was surely a street from a ghost town—shrouded in gray and eerily silent.

The story reversed itself when I drove back to the houses along Perry and Huron Streets, a block from the water, where my grandparents and other relatives had lived. I had feared I would find these in disrepair, perhaps even swept into Lake Erie since waves and storms had been assaulting the rocks at the end of the street for years. Instead, I found a newly designated Historic District with signs on some of the refurbished houses announcing their original owners. People were outside pounding nails and repainting as I drove up. I don't think I imagined it. It was like a movie location with technical crews setting up for the action to come.

As I parked the car, out of nowhere a gray-haired guide appeared who seemed for all the world as though she had been expecting me. I never quite registered her name, but she recognized my name immediately (had even known my father). She lived next to the old Tuttle house, she told me, and began walking with me explaining who had bought this one, and who that, and which were for sale and how much they were asking. The Swenson house near the lake was one of those marked with a sign. This Swedish couple was famous for crumb and crème cakes (kuchen) from their bakery on Main Street. My guide knew that, also, and assured me those could still be purchased from their grandchildren in a new location.

My grandparents' house looked terrific: fresh paint, porches newly enclosed and extended, with ladders, trestles, and cans of paint visible through the window of the old sunroom. It was soon to go up for sale, my guide told me. My heart leaped, and for a long, tempting minute, I almost determined to live there. I imagined myself hearing again the constant murmur of the lake, walking the sidewalks with their peculiar rippled concrete to the beach a block away.

The huge Lee house next door was now a bed-and-breakfast trimmed in ornate Victorian curlicues, painted lavender and pink. It sported a new porch, and what looked to be valets were running around helping people with luggage. Maybe I imagined that, too. People seemed to be swarming around the entire area like Keebler elves.

At the end of the street by the lake, which I approached cautiously, expecting to see a sharp drop and waves crashing, I found a quiet, little well-kept park that my guide explained was actually public, although the owners of the end property liked for people to believe it was theirs. I sat on their bench, and bidding goodbye to my guide, watched the sunlight reflecting on the perfectly calm, soothing water as a beautiful young girl in a sports bra and running shorts appeared, walking a large Old English sheepdog through the private/public new park atop the rocks at the end of the street.

When I had collected what was left of my sense of reality, I drove to the eastern edge of town to seek out the places where my mother and I had spent our summers all those decades ago. Among new fast-food restaurants, motels, and summer home developments, traces could still be found. The dance hall at Crystal Beach was, of course, gone—had been for decades, as was the amusement park, but Nokomis Park still existed. I couldn't find "the Shack" where my mother and I had lived, but Molly's house at the end of the street was still there with a stranger mowing the lawn. The steep staircase to the beach had disappeared, and as I discovered when I cautiously crept to the top of the rocks, the beach as well. Lake Erie had had one victory at least over my past.

As a final gesture, I negotiated the frightening drive to the river bottom where old Acorn Lodge had sat. Of course, the drive was not nearly as rugged as I had believed, and the low-rent river bottom had been yuppified and gentrified into a sparkling new marina, campground, and resort. On the spot where Acorn Lodge had sat was a contemporary cabin on stilts painted in a metallic teal color in a nest of similar structures designed to withstand the periodic flooding for which that area was known. When I had lived there in the fifties, we had tied a rope to a tree on the hill behind the cabin in order to climb up to the road above and visit with friends on the heights. Like an idiot, I got out of the car expecting to find that rope. Only in my imagination.

Before I left Vermilion, I stopped at the location once known as McGarvey's Restaurant, nestled under the drawbridge between the lagoons and the river.

McGarvey's had served seafood, and liquor, and provided along its wharf gasoline pumps for boaters. It was an institution in its day, full of friendly people enjoying themselves. It is now called the Red Clay on the River after the color of the clay along the riverbanks that had given Vermilion its name. It was a different building, the foyer filled with pictures of the old McGarvey's and the fire that had destroyed it some time ago. The menu was updated, but as I relaxed in a deck chair on the porch enjoying glazed salmon and a glass of chardonnay, I watched people climbing out of their boats, talking fishing and sailing, drinking and laughing with the same conviviality of old. I almost expected to see Uncle Dave enter and start working the room as only he could do.

I sat there through a long twilight, alone in the crowd with my wineglass, watching the boats pass up and down by the new condominiums where the old Kishman Fish House had been. I felt the companionship of a lone seagull as he sat on a post nearby watching with me, occasionally stretching his wings and settling back again—reluctant to fly away. I don't think I have been in Vermilion for the last time.

Values in Transition

*M*y husband, Jon, and I went to liberal-arts colleges at a time when higher education was not pursued in order to obtain a well-paying job. This is a notion totally incomprehensible to any student I ever taught from the mid-seventies until I retired.

"If you didn't go so you could get a good job, Ms. Mezz, then why *did* you go?"

"I went to become an educated person." I would reply. "Think about that."

I have been thinking about that often since I came back to Ohio. I find as I sort through physical and emotional baggage from my past, I must also sift through the values I believe to be true and wisdom upon which I depend. As I interact with people, listen to the news, I sense my opinions forming, my priorities settling into their customary places, and I wonder, "How did I come to believe that?" These days, in the climate of the nation's well-publicized cultural divides, I also have to wonder which of my values stem from my small-town upbringing and which I have brought back with me as a result of my experiences in college and beyond.

One concept I can trace directly to my education is the idea that life is a constant journey leading to the discovery of new beliefs and perceptions. It took me a while to understand that not everybody sees it that way. Many people, and not just those in small-town America, settle on their beliefs early in life and cling to them like a lifeboat through hell and high water. I have never been comfortable with the idea of an absolute truth—not growing up, certainly not now—except perhaps the truth of the journey itself. A belief in the inevitability of change, discovery, and the perpetual process of learning is as close as I will ever come to a leap of faith, a premise at the base of all else. "Whatever happens," Jon always tells me, "is okay if you can grow from it." And so we both believed when young, and so we still believe like a mantra running through our minds, as constant as the rhythm of breathing.

When we moved to Ohio from California, we tried to use the occasion to unload much of the detritus that collects over a lifetime. We were only partially successful. It wasn't difficult to discard clothes and kitchenware, but when it came to books and music, the process was excruciating. I would take an old textbook or collection of plays in hand, ready to stuff into the paper bag for the used bookstore, and—the process would short-circuit. Either he or I would pause, remember, and place it instead in the box to take with us. "I think I would like to read that just one more time," one of us would say. Revisit that particular discovery, recall a once new idea one more time before moving on again.

So we brought them with us—our educations. The beliefs, perceptions, and values collected over decades of classes, books, and the experiences of life. Because Jon copes with multiple sclerosis, such recollections have proved to be a solace in the isolation of illness. For me, it has been much more complex.

The California writer Richard Rodriguez, whose books and *Los Angeles Times* articles I always eagerly devoured, coined a phrase to describe himself whenever he returned to his parents' home from graduate work at UC–Berkeley. He said the experience of returning to his cultural roots, education in tow, was akin to becoming an "anthropologist in the family kitchen." Everything once natural, viewed un-self-consciously from the inside, now appeared altered in the harsh light of detachment and analysis. It is a gain in understanding, but a hurtful loss of innocence and the sense of belonging. And so it was for me on my rare visits back. I was afraid it might be so again, but magically, it is not.

Most certainly, I am not the girl I was when I left. I have been urbanized, politicized, and liberated from the presumptions I grew up with. My tastes in music, decor, clothing, and cuisine are drastically different now, and I have had experiences I hesitate to reveal to 90 percent of the people I meet here. I have come home with Jon, a Jewish New Yorker, who reminds me every day where we have been. We don't enjoy church suppers or dances at the Eagles on Saturday nights, and we prefer professional basketball to local or college games (perhaps the worst heresy of all). But it doesn't matter. Because my education hasn't really stopped. In fact, it continues more intensely than ever before. And this is what I am learning.

There is still a place for me here, a place prepared decades, perhaps even centuries ago. This is truly the only place in the world where, as Robert Frost wrote "When you have to go there, they have to take you in." No matter what you have become. A small town truly does embrace its own. Preble County embraced my great-grandfather Allen Garber, with his long beard and Dunkard beliefs; it tolerated my grandfather Otha Hecathorn, in spite of the fact that he was a Democrat and an intellectual whose favorite entertainment was playing with a slide rule on long winter evenings. Eaton accepted my mother when she walked the tightrope at the Famous Preble County Fair and through who knows what other shenanigans. And it will embrace me as well because I have a right to be here—whatever I have become.

So I am looking again at what I believe—looking again at the town where I grew up from the perspective of where I started and through the prism of all the places I have been and the things I have learned. I expect to be a lot more educated in a few years than I have ever been before.

Faith of My Grandfathers

Since I reached retirement, I feel compelled to allocate days of the week to particular activities. On Friday morning I shop for groceries. It is a luxury to shop on a weekday and avoid the crowds. My fellow shoppers now are housewives, retirees, and other persons not in the workforce. Often among them are several German Baptist (Dunkard) women. I am fascinated. I sneak peeks at what they put in their carts, at their dress and demeanor. My cousin Benny confessed to me the same curiosity. "There but for the grace of God," I said. Perhaps I should have said, "There if I were truly possessed of the grace of God."

A German Baptist is the Eaton version of the more familiar Amish, a religious sect that, although formed almost two hundred years after the Amish, sprang out of the same dedication to pacifism, plain living, and nonconformity to the wider world. Of course, my cousin and I are especially fascinated by the Dunkards because our ancestors on our mothers' side were members of that sect, farmed in the traditional fashion, and wore the distinguishing garb. Our great-grandfather Allen Garber was the nearest ancestor to practice the faith. After him the family attended the Congregational Christian Church, now known as the United Church of Christ.

Among the Protestant churches, it is often difficult for any outsider to know what separates one from another. At least with the German Baptists, one can be sure who they are. They look different; they live differently. They wear their faith for all to see.

My curiosity drove me to study the history of the German Baptists and other similar sects. In books they are usually grouped together under the name Anabaptist (for one reason because they reject infant baptism). Anabaptists first appeared in the earliest days of the Protestant Reformation when the barn doors of the Catholic Church were forced open and new interpretations of worship and the Bible came pouring out like herds of horses fleeing a fire. It was inevitable that some souls, once impelled to put their own interpretation on the example of the life of Christ, would choose to shun worldly ways and gather together with others of common belief to live apart from what they perceived as the general immorality of the times.

I have always loved the outspoken language of this passage from *The Garber Historical and Genealogical Record*: "The history of the Garber family over the past four hundred years began with the Reformation and its attendant debauchery, persecutions and destruction of innocent families by the pandering, inhumane servants of the Catholic Church." Everybody, it seems, persecuted the Anabaptists whether they came to be called Mennonite, Amish, or Old Order German Baptist Brethren. The barn doors of the Catholic Church were open, but by no means did the Protestant Reformation signal true freedom of worship. Luther himself was quite unforgiving about nonconformists, as were the hundreds of kings, dukes, princes, landgraves, and clerics who jostled over what should be the official religion of each duchy, principality, or city in the vast Germanic territories.

As Catholics, Lutherans, and Calvinists divided the spoils of the religious wars among themselves over several centuries, the Anabaptists, although consistently paragons of morality, were at the bottom of everyone's pecking order. For their refusal to conform, they were banished, chased, thrown in rivers with their feet tied to drown, imprisoned, burned at the stake, and condemned to the galleys to perish as slaves. Hounded from place to place, they searched for sympathetic local rulers who might be, if not openly supportive, at least indifferent enough to their existence to allow them a modicum of privacy in their beliefs. In that way their history resembles that of the Jews.

Often, the only reason the Anabaptists were tolerated was that, as superlative farmers, they were able to restore the land to productivity in countries ravaged by war. Although some must have renounced their beliefs, many thousands were true martyrs marching stalwartly to their death with pride and conviction in their sure salvation. No wonder they escaped to the New World as soon as they learned of its existence.

In America the various groups of Anabaptists suffered some intimidation from irate veterans of both the Revolutionary and Civil Wars who resented the fact that they were pacifist, and therefore, continued to prosper on the land while others were answering the call to battle. However, for the most part, they have been left alone to maintain their traditional lives and take their place as throwbacks to the distant past. They keep to themselves, remain wary of the world, and find ways to survive in spite of rapidly changing conditions in farming, their traditional means of support. I see the women, of late, peddling homemade noodles, bread, or pastry in real estate offices. I also see many of them working in stores and places of business, even in hospitals.

There has been, apparently, some loosening of the rules, since recently I have noticed they drive pickup trucks and minivans of all colors instead of the undecorated black vehicles I remember. But the dress remains the same: white or black caps for the women covering hair brushed back from the forehead and gathered into a bun and long-sleeved, cotton print dresses with wraparound skirt buttoned down the front with a covering cape. The men are often in work clothes or overalls, almost always bearded with a distinctive haircut cropped off at the neck.

As I watch Dunkard women in the supermarket on Friday mornings, I struggle to find some way to identify. I know I share more genes with these women than with almost anyone in New York City, for instance. I also know, having studied their traditions, that shreds of their beliefs and experience continue in me. These are people, like the Quakers, who know with a searing, deadly sense of reality, underscored by the blood of their predecessors, why a government should never again be allowed to promote a religion or interfere with its practice in any way. They also understand, as did my pacifist Quaker teachers at Earlham College, the absolute evil of war and violence, especially wars fought under the name of God, by whatever name God is called. And they possess, almost from birth, the courage required to sustain a moral conviction through any kind of torture or ridicule, against any law or government to the contrary or social expectation. I cannot help but take pride in having been both descended from and educated by such people.

I envy the constant cheerfulness of these women, as well as the strong, supportive sense of community they enjoy. But most of all, I love the simplicity of their lives, almost monastic in their avoidance of objects of vanity or personal show. I think as I look at their plain faces and dress, "That part of it I could do." It would be a relief to rid my life of the useless clutter of possessions, reroute the mind to matters much less trivial. This was, in fact, one of my goals, and Jon's, when we returned to this rural place—a shedding of the trappings of the more materialistic lifestyle of a city. A craving for a time when I could stop, as I did this morning while walking the dog, to watch the forsythia bloom or follow birdsong among the trees. When Jon could sit on the back porch and listen to the rustle of leaves rather than the constant hum of traffic on a city street. In the words of the Shaker song. "'Tis the gift to be simple. 'Tis the gift to be free. 'Tis the gift to come down where we ought to be." Still.

A Dunkard woman is checking out groceries at the supermarket. I know she is still new at the job since she looked up the code numbers for almost every item. On occasion, I have made purchases that stymied the women—usually, unfamiliar city items such as pine nuts or radicchio. This time the Dunkard cashier held up one of my purchases and said, "What are these?" They were limes. The other checkers rolled their eyes.

Much as I admire their moral courage, much as I envy the simple lives of the German Baptist Brethren, much as I know I could pack all my possessions in a box and give them away; in the final analysis, I would not seek to live among them. I find there are things I pity as well. I pity the smallness of their world fenced in by taboo and suspicion. I found that trait in my grandmother Nina, who distrusted and ultimately rejected anyone whose ancestry she did not know. I pity their disregard for man-made beauty, of art and design, cuisine, music and literature, which rival nature in their capacity to soothe, please, and inspire. And, most of all, I pity the ironic conformity required in a community of non-conformists that prescribes dress, lifestyle, and habits of behavior. I believe that such conformity stifles and frustrates many individual dreams and hopes, especially among the young.

Simplicity can be a treacherous concept, I am finding, and "coming down where we ought to be" not quickly learned.

Shadow Memories

I understand people who are fascinated with psychology and the mysteries of the human mind. Sometimes my own mind feels momentarily like a catacomb, a labyrinth of twisting caves, rocky dead ends, and threatening shapes that flicker across dimly lit, moist walls or scurry around corners at the fringes of sight, as in a fantasy computer game in which an orc, goblin, or a skeleton might suddenly appear and spring into battle. I know there are people who spend time stumbling through such labyrinths seeking terrible memories that desperately need to be dragged into the bright light aboveground.

Fortunately for me, no unbearable horrors lurk in the dungeon of my mind, yet I would never discount the powerful effect of my own shadow memories on my beliefs and values. Nature or nurture be damned, the experiences of childhood are the first and strongest imprints on the stuff of a mind, and if any of us really wants to understand why he or she is inclined one way or another in attitude, creed, or philosophy, it is necessary to travel there—to that catacomb—at least for a little while. For me, that journey is infinitely easier to make now that I have before me every day the sensory trigger of the sights, sounds, and smells of this place, the very place where those memories were imprinted decades ago. Memories that share the irrationality of dreams, and sometimes appear to be indistinguishable from them:

> Behind most of the houses that line the streets of Eaton are backyards and alleys that make wonderful shortcuts when walking home from school or playing games in the neighborhood. In one of those alleys while going home one day, I came upon two girls from one of the two

or three black families who lived in Eaton. They were being taunted by neighborhood bullies. Pebbles were thrown—perhaps a rock—the word *nigger* was shouted, and one of the boys urinated on an alley fence as a gesture of humiliation. The girls escaped, angry tears rolling down their faces, and I scurried home in the other direction in shock, feeling as though it had happened to me.

When President Roosevelt died in 1945, my mother heard it first on the radio. "Go out." she said, "And tell your grandmother." Nina was in the garden, a garden we knew as the victory garden because during World War II everyone was encouraged to grow as much of their own food as they could to help in the war effort. I was only five or six, but I remember this more clearly than anything else from those days. Nina sat down in the dirt and wept, tears tracing through the soil on her hands. From that time on, although I didn't know then what a Democrat was, I knew I was one, in spite of the fact that being Democrats seemed to make us somehow different in my hometown.

My father was in the navy during World War II. When he came home on leave, Mother and I went to Virginia, to meet the ship, even though, by then, my parents were separated, soon to be officially divorced. I was small and overtired, and I headed for a nearby bench to sit down. My father grabbed me by the arm and pulled me off. "You can't sit there." It was a "Colored Only" bench. My mother grabbed me back again and sat me down. "She'll sit there if she wants to." she said. Since I was a little white girl sitting on a "colored bench," rather than a black girl sitting on a "white bench" the situation was more than a little backward. But I got the point.

Brenda Baumhart Mezz

Charley in uniform during World War II.

The Place Just Right

As I relive these memories now, I realize just how much growing up in the forties and fifties molded me to become part of the idealistic sixties generation—honed my sympathies for minorities. The influences were just the right balance of good and bad. On the one hand, examples of racial stereotypes and repression were abundant in Eaton as they were all over America in those suspicious, paranoid Cold War days. I look at some of my children's books, and negative images of Asian people and Blacks are all over them, even in *Mary Poppins*. Nobody thought a thing about that, but *The Catcher in the Rye* and *Lady Chatterley's Lover* were banned. Sex was underground, and profanity brought disapproving frowns—except, of course, for my Uncle Buzz, who always said "God damn" whenever he felt like it and was loved in spite of it.

On the other hand, examples of tolerance and generosity were also abundant. My mother never considered herself a radical, but she had a soft heart for a hard-luck case. The whole family did. They practiced charity—toward the neglected children my social-worker aunt, Eleanor, would rescue, as well as toward the Appalachian transplants whose simple writing and colorful expressions my mother praised and cherished as an English teacher. When years later Cousin Sarah brought home for Thanksgiving a young black parolee from her job as a probation officer, it wasn't at all strange to us.

Even my mother's parents, Nina and Otha, had taken in two homeless girls during the hard times of the thirties, and for several years when I was very little, the two north rooms in 824 North Maple Street belonged to Mrs. Stubbs, an elderly woman who apparently had nowhere else to live. I don't know about other families—perhaps it was simply the generosity of typical small-town Americans who had learned to help each other through the Depression—but it was a natural thing to help the downtrodden in those days. Even in my father's Republican family.

When Grandmother Frances died, a veritable parade of people, from a variety of religions and several ethnicities, came to tell of various deeds she had quietly done for them. Sometimes it had been money given, more often acceptance, kindness, and respect when such virtues were scarce. It seemed to me then that the only difference between a conservative and a liberal, between a Republican and a Democrat, was not the presence or absence of charitable feelings, but how close and personal someone was willing to be about it. My grandfather Baumhart, in a fine Republican tradition, lent money to the doctor to establish his practice, and even to the Japanese Mr. Okagi for his restaurant (an astounding act to me given the fact that it was so close to World War II). Democrats Otha and Nina took in strays and invited them to the breakfast table.

It is risky to delve too deeply into shadow memories. The rivers of childhood impressions run swiftly by, and the stepping stones by which to cross are covered with slippery gray-green moss. There is no bridge to hold to, no signs to distinguish between a surety and a hope, a fact and a fearsome dream, a truth and a wish. Yet, ultimately, what difference does it make? Real or imaginary or some of each, this is the psychic stuff we accumulate—and I am not likely to replace it with contrary experiences or become capable of being argued out of it. For better or worse, it has helped make me who I am. I am forever grateful for the people, the places, and the times that made my shadow world, in spite of my own orcs and ghouls, more sweet than sad, more good than evil, more generous than spiteful, more loving than hateful.

Losing My Religion

Last Wednesday was the first meeting of the Lakengren Women's Club after the winter hiatus. Along with the Alpha Garden Club, I attend the Lakengren Women's Club to stay in touch with my surroundings. In this case, I mean my immediate surroundings here at Lake Lakengren, the small development/resort/retirement community about four miles south of Eaton where Jon and I live. These ladies, having come from many other places, are much less likely to have known my mother, but more likely to be the ones who wave from their cars as I walk the dog.

During an interlude between the business meeting and the presentation of the results of the silent auction, a woman in the row of folding chairs behind me suddenly blurted out, "You look just like a woman who goes to my church! Do you belong to the Church of the Visitation?"

"No," I answered, somewhat startled. "But I guess I could look like other people around here. It's probably the same gene pool."

"It's amazing," she insisted. "Same hair color, same size. You could be twins. What church do you go to?"

Now I really was startled. I had been dreading that question since I moved here, but after all these months, this was the first time anyone had actually asked. And in public, too, with at least a dozen people listening. "Uh," I replied. "I don't really go to church." Then, after an awkward pause, "When I was growing up, I was a member of the United Church of Christ on Decatur Street." The results of the silent auction began, so I guess I was saved, so to speak. My secret remained hidden.

The truth is I lost my belief in the God I grew up with shortly before my high-school graduation while attending Girls State in Columbus. Girls State is an annual gathering of selected high-school students (there is also a Boys State) to learn the political process through a mock legislative session on-site in the state capitol. My social-studies teacher, Mr. Williams, recommended me, I think, because I liked to argue in class. For him, arguing was a positive thing. Most other teachers, including my mother, considered it disrespectful.

At Girls State we were housed in an Ohio State University dormitory full of argumentative young people chosen, like me, for that very quality. Most were even more opinionated and strident than I was, and as I soon learned, considerably more exposed and knowledgeable. My religion was challenged by a determined, gruff young woman whose name, I believe, was Marion. In about an hour and a half she punched my feeble religious dogma so full of holes logically that it disappeared forever. I simply had no answers to her barrage of Socratic questions.

Afterward, as I lay in my top bunk in that stuffy dormitory room, I felt as though I had been ravaged. I had lost not only an argument, but my innocence as well; and worse, the friendly, comforting God I had envisioned all my life, the grandfatherly personage with the white beard and kindly, human-like face, had evaporated. I was devastated. I was adrift in space spinning out of the reach of gravity into nothingness. It was terrifying. I spent the night not in sleep, but in despair, holding on to the edges of that top bunk lest my body fly after my mind into a vortex of empty, indifferent ether.

That must have been when the anger began—anger not at Marion or at the universe, but at my family and teachers—anger that I had been so duped by the people and community who professed to love me. It was an anger I was to carry for most of my life, normally carefully contained, but occasionally spilling out in venomous rudeness to missionaries at the front door, biting sarcasm at ministers on the airways, and exasperated ridicule of crowds pouring out of churches on Sunday mornings, creating congestion as I ventured out for a paper or a casual breakfast at a restaurant.

I've calmed down—some—over the years. Obviously, nobody intended to dupe or embarrass me. Almost everybody sent his or her children to church when I was growing up in Eaton, and, undoubtedly, still does today. It would never have occurred to my mother in a million years that I would bitterly resent it for the rest of my life.

The religious doctrine set forth by the Congregational Christian Church (later the United Church of Christ) was not difficult to comprehend. My religious instruction began with my singing "Jesus Loves Me," "Jesus Wants Me for a Sunbeam," and "The B-I-B-L-E." (Yes that's the book for me). I once heard this described as the Little Golden Book approach to God. The really important impressions seemed to come through the hymns and pictures, just as in the Middle Ages.

I came to see God in the humanized image of Michelangelo's Jehovah. I saw Jesus through Da Vinci's *Last Supper*, a gentle, kindly man with a sweet face and shoulder-length reddish hair. Either or both of them could be called upon in any emergency and were to be treated as confidants in prayer. They would "abide with me" and walk with me "in the garden." I was expected to establish a personal relationship with these images, and they would give me strength to get through any kind of grief, along with the support of my fellow believers.

In return I had to love my fellow man, be a good girl, and, most important, have faith—just believe, and all would be well. After a life of this, I would then go to heaven, or hell if I had sinned. It had to be pretty terrible, however, because God and his son, Jesus, were very forgiving. The Congregational Christian Church didn't try to scare us with hellfire and damnation as did the Holy Rollers, for whom my family had much disdain. It was pretty tacky to rant and rave as they reputedly did in their long, intense services. In the Congregational Christian Church we were tasteful and dignified. It was also, at least as I look back on it today, bland, superficial, and sanitized.

It didn't take much punching and testing for my fellow Girls Stater Marion to topple this rather simplistic construct. Most of it could be summed up in the phrase "Prove it," followed by searing questions such as: "Where did this God come from?" and "Why do other cultures worship different Gods?" The key, I finally realized, was, obviously, faith. Blindly trusting was the only way to know the truth of any of it, and even in those days, I knew my skeptical mind would never be capable of such trust. To my way of thinking, I might as well put my faith in fairies, leprechauns, and unicorns. There wasn't much difference when it all came out in the wash. And that was that.

Provincial

There are three good ways to get from Eaton to Richmond, Indiana, sixteen miles to the west. Strangers to the area usually drive seven miles north along State Route 127 to exit 10 at the interstate where, just past the budget motel and truck stop, they can turn west and be there in practically no time at all.

Carpenters and other workmen (of which there are many in this working-class community) speed their way along a variety of county roads, past farms and tiny crossroads communities such as Campbellstown or West Florence, to the lumber, plumbing, or discount home stores along the eastern edge of Richmond. But most people just head out Route 35, known as the Richmond Pike in Eaton and the Eaton Pike in Richmond. Most citizens in Eaton go to Richmond regularly. For all the pride Eatonians have in the smallness and unspoiled serenity of their little town, many things they all need can't be found within its borders: good restaurants, movies, and shopping—the services of hospitals, medical specialists, and orthodontists. Lord knows, Richmond is no Cincinnati with its theaters, museums, and other urban delights, but it will do when you just have to get to Lowe's.

Most Eatonians, however, seldom travel to the western edge of Richmond where, nestled next to a cemetery on the southern side of the Old National Trail Road (Route 40), the campus of Earlham College is located. Maybe that's because, as I learned, the journey from Eaton to Earlham may be twenty miles in distance, but closer to twenty thousand in consciousness. This was especially true when I quietly moved my belongings into an Earlham dormitory in the waning years of the uncomplicated fifties. A Quaker school with deep pacifist and international concerns, steeped in liberal thinking and highly idealistic, Earlham provided a very early transition into the consciousness associated with the sixties, an exposure that changed me forever. I would never again be the provincial small-town girl I had been in the days when a carload of us from Eaton High School would drive over and circle the road around the grassy "Heart" in the middle of campus, yelling "Thee" and "Thou," our ignorant attempt to ridicule Quakers.

Although I didn't know I was provincial (I expect no one ever does, by definition), I had an early sense there were things in the world, wonderful things, I just couldn't see, much less understand. I once saw a movie in which a glamorous but mysterious lady appeared at a funeral in a huge hat, her face behind a thick veil. For some reason I remembered and identified with that image. The glamorous part of it was, I suppose, only wishful thinking because the true mystery was not the identity of the woman, but what she could possibly be seeing under that thick veil. The material made the world foggy, and the brim hid most of it from view. Like that lady's my visible world was limited, constricted and tunnel-visioned. It frustrated me then, and later, as things became clearer, embarrassed me as well.

A small Midwestern town in the forties and early fifties offered few glimpses into a larger reality. Unlike today when television and other electronic media give every grade-schooler a sophisticated image of the globe, Eaton, Ohio, in the forties lived in pristine, rural isolation. I saw my mother and grandmother, with whom I lived. I saw the "other side" of the family on holidays. I saw the modest rooms of my house on the corner of Maple and Mechanic Streets, and the tree-drenched roads and sidewalks of my town. I saw the schoolroom with its scarred wooden desks and creaky stairs and the cornfields and woods from the window of our black Chevy. But I was twelve when I first discovered the joys of radio soap opera, fourteen before I saw Milton Berle on television.

It was still possible in those days to find people who had no concept of a life beyond the next county. When he joined the army, my college friend Fred, from Kansas, told his aunt and uncle down on the farm he was going to Germany. "Is that on past Wichita?" they wanted to know. My grandma Nina (pronounced with a long *i* sound not long *e*) was not much more aware of the world.

As for millions of children before me—since the dawn of civilization, if writers are to be believed—my salvation was books. I read constantly, night and day: under my covers with the proverbial flashlight, on the beach near my father's town in the blazing hot sun, mindless of sunburn or glare. I read the Oz books, all of them. I read Nancy Drew and the Bobbsey Twins. I read comic books and lengthy instructions from prescription bottles. It was totally undirected and obsessive reading, but it did its job.

It began to open my mind to possibilities beyond the limits of rural Ohio, as well as to provide stimulating if conflicting insights into human relations. By the time I was ready to go to college, I had read my way through my mother's master's degree reading assignments, including (unbeknownst to her) an exceptionally adult series of books (James T. Farrell's *Studs Lonigan*, for instance) in Modern American Literature from which I obtained my earliest education about sex.

In my senior year in high school I began to understand how underexposed to the world I really was and to catch a glimpse of what might have been had I been reared somewhere else. I had occasion to be with a small group of people my own age from Dayton (the big city for us). These kids were the cream of the crop for their time, most from exceptionally fine schools, sons and daughters of people far richer and more sophisticated than I could imagine. We had all been chosen by the *Dayton Daily News* as representative young people, and they used us to give opinions on "young people's issues" in a series of public forums, panel discussions, and articles. They also took us to Washington, D.C., in the spring as a reward. I was the token representative from the outlying readership area, or so I think now.

The group was infinitely more "cool" than my friends from Eaton. Music, for instance, was part of their lives and preoccupation, not just background noise. Their reading was focused and actually chosen because they were familiar with the writer or because they knew the ideas they were looking for would be there. They had like-minded companions to talk with about "serious issues" and "important events." They were, most of all, socially adept and could use a finger bowl if required and choose the proper clothes for the proper occasion. They were nice enough and friendly, but they made me feel, as Grandma Nina would have said, like something the cat dragged in.

The Place Just Right

I wonder if the staff of Earlham College had any idea in 1957, when I moved into Olvey-Andis Hall, how provincial this freshman really was, and how far it actually was from Eaton to that campus south of the Old National Trail Road in Richmond, Indiana.

I suspect it was no surprise to them.

Part II

'TIS THE GIFT TO BE GENTLE
'TIS THE GIFT TO BE FAIR
'TIS THE GIFT TO WAKE
AND BREATHE THE MORNING AIR.
TO WALK EVERY DAY

IN THE PATH WE CHOOSE

'TIS THE GIFT THAT WE PRAY
WE NEVER, NEVER LOSE

The Alpha Garden Club Visits a Cemetery

For the muggy August 2003 meeting, instead of the usual lunch and program, the Alpha Garden Club opted for a field trip to the Cox Arboretum and living butterfly exhibit in Dayton. However, much to the dismay of past president Grace Rust, who was in charge of the activity, the plans fell through because of new construction at the arboretum and a lack of available vehicles in which our less athletic members might be transported along the roads. At our ages, such amenities become very important to the enjoyment of an outing. Therefore, Grace arranged for us to go to the Woodland Cemetery instead.

Woodland Cemetery, a verdant oasis centrally located in old Dayton, has been much in the news of late because it harbors the graves of the Wright family: Orville, Wilbur, and their parents and some of their siblings. Neil Armstrong, John Glenn, and other innovators in the field of aviation helped conduct a widely broadcast ceremony at the Wright gravesite as an important part of the centennial celebration of the invention of flight.

The ladies of the Alpha Garden Club, after lunch and a short meeting at the MCL Cafeteria traveled through Woodland Cemetery in their own vehicles. We were led by Barbara, our guide in the first car who spoke to all of us through walkie-talkies, which didn't crackle too much after the first few minutes. I rode with Ruth Ann, current president and new/old friend. We had a few chuckles at the walkie-talkie conversations aimed at getting everyone at the right volume level with the right buttons pushed.

"Barbara, you're going in and out!"

"You have to point it a certain direction…"

"Are you pointing it?"

"Barbara, you're going in and out!"

At the Wright grave site we left the cars and walked, some of us offering arms to others, down the steep, grassy hillside to the actual graves. A few wreaths on easels were still standing from the ceremony, and people had left pennies scattered all over the modest headstones. On Wilbur's headstone was placed one of the new Ohio bicentennial quarters with a picture of the first airplane etched in the middle.

After the official ceremonies had been aired on television and vanished into the clouds, ordinary people had chosen this way to show their respect. In fact, while we were there, a very young couple wandered up talking about a project on the Wrights they were doing at school. They stood in apparent awe for a few minutes, seemingly surprised that the Wright brothers' bones were actually present. It's a jolt to realize you are in the proximity of genuine legends, even if they are long dead. I remembered my uncle Ben telling me that he often saw Orville wandering into the Dayton bank where Ben worked in the mid-forties. Ben didn't think too much of it then. That gives me two degrees of separation from seeing the man myself. Not too bad.

On the way up the hill, back to the cars, we stopped at the headstone of Paul Laurence Dunbar, the black poet who is another icon of the history of Dayton. An icon of an entirely different sort. His remains lie under a willow tree, a poem about "restin 'neath a willow" on a plaque nearby. Sarah, a former teacher, who often voluntarily shares poetry with the Alpha Garden Club, remarked that when she was teaching during the sixties, she was criticized for including Paul Laurence Dunbar in her lessons. At first I thought she meant there had been racists who disrespected black writers. But she explained that the criticism, from many parents, was that the dialect in which Dunbar deliberately wrote, full of old-fashioned Black English, disrespected and demeaned blacks in general. Something, I guess, like the criticism of the Uncle Remus stories also common in those days. She found it hard to understand. She thought the poems were beautiful as they were.

Finally, before heading home, we entered the mausoleum to view the stained-glass windows. Although the principal windows were on Christian themes, several were devoted to poetry; in particular, Henry Wadsworth Longfellow's *Evangeline* and *The Song of Hiawatha*. Grace's husband, Willie, is interred there, and we read the stone face of the vault where he lay. He had been there since 1974. Her name was there, too, without dates, of course, since she was standing among us very much alive. I thought it must feel eerie to be gazing at your own death vault, your name already carved, a vault waiting patiently for your mortal remains. But Grace didn't seem to find it strange. Maybe when you are ninety-four, there is some security in knowing where you will rest and by whom.

There is nothing like a day at a cemetery, among the famous and not-so-famous departed, to set a mind wondering what it is that is important about a human life.

Now that my working life is over and the final (hopefully, long and active) phase of living has begun, it seems appropriate for me to pay attention to what was important about mine as I passed through the long years getting to this place and time. Important both personally and in the larger scheme of things. So far I don't see anything to warrant a plaque on a stone under a willow tree—certainly not a headstone strewn with pennies. But it will be enough if I can find more to be proud of than ashamed.

Besides, I have some distance to go. Maybe I can still do something memorable. You never know.

Worth Doing

When I was very young, idealistic, and obnoxiously full of myself, I wrote in the back of a philosophy book a short list of things worth doing in life. The book was by Bertrand Russell, with whom I once felt a great affinity, although I would be hard-pressed now to explain his system of belief. I do remember he was in the forefront of the antiwar movement, and he believed in a mind free from traditional religious thinking. Both of those positions, as the Quakers used to say, "spoke to my condition" in those days.

Russell was also famous as a logician, as I recall, which must explain how I could have believed questions so large could be reduced to propositions so few. I brazenly determined then, loosely based on the traditional categories of the liberal arts, that three areas of endeavor gave a person a shot at doing something of value to better the world.

The first area, as in the example of Orville and Wilbur Wright, was the discovery of knowledge—i.e., science, invention, and scholarship. The second was good works such as teaching, medicine, or social work; and the last was creativity—poetry and the arts. Back then, in the sixties, it was often implied that doing almost anything else, particularly if it was in support of the military-industrial complex, was not only not worthwhile but morally suspect. These, of course, were the years when the counterculture was forming, when it was becoming fashionable to "turn on, tune in, drop out."

Long after that little volume by Bertrand Russell disappeared, I have remembered that list. I realize now it was more prediction than plan. I have indeed spent all my life studying, teaching, or trying to practice an art. To be honest, I did not always choose my work because I was consciously trying to do something of value for the world. I was just not suited for anything else—too timid to be

The Place Just Right

competitive in business, too passive to fight, clueless and disinterested when it came to making money.

To most of the hardworking, practical people by whom I was and am again surrounded in Eaton—to the contractors, farmers and factory workers, the grocers, filling-station operators, waitresses, and insurance salesmen, I know my youthful concept of what is worth doing is from somewhere across a great mental and experiential divide.

I have heard it said that the sixties generation was privileged to follow lofty goals because their practical parents had sacrificed during the Depression and two world wars to make such idealism possible. Liberated from economic uncertainty, my generation was free to dabble in areas (social protest, for instance, or the arts) not normally rewarded with regular paychecks or considered especially useful to daily survival. If so, it was a rare window of opportunity because it wasn't like that for long. By the mid-seventies most young people were occupied again in training for the good job, too scared of being left out of the marketplace to get serious about philosophy, the fine arts, or even poorly paid jobs in social services. And I think, except for a small but constant percentage of unspoiled idealists in some liberal-arts colleges, it remains that way to this day.

Somehow, I slipped into adulthood through that timely window. Not many, if any, of my classmates at Eaton High School had the same experience. My mother, herself a graduate of Earlham College, had become an enthusiastic believer in the broadening influence of the liberal arts, so she saw to it that I followed in her footsteps. She was the exception. The small number of my classmates who even went to college went to career-oriented state universities. While they were working at or preparing for a job or enlisting in the military, I was reading Plato, Ibsen, and Bertrand Russell. While they advanced in a career and raised families, I subsisted on graduate assistantships (plentiful in those days) and studied playwriting and acting. When they were getting ready to send their own children to college, I was still living like a struggling artist in a run-down rented cottage in Los Angeles, hanging around theaters and theater people. I could describe it as not losing my ideals; some people around here might call it not growing up.

Until I was forty-five years old, when I began my high-school teaching career kicking and screaming as though I were being dragged by demons into hell, I lived around people who pitied all the other poor souls living in the "real world" or the "straight world" in contrast, for instance, to the academic ivory tower or to the theater world. Having to enter the "real" or "straight" world was something to be dreaded. In that place, survival was the purpose and nine to five the means. It represented the end of all dreams, the beginning of defeat and compromise—a capitulation to the mundane, the crass, and, worst of all, the boring.

At the age of forty-five I found myself in a midlife crisis that had nothing to do with menopause, libido, unfulfilled dreams, or wasted years. Because of Jon's MS, for the first time in my life, I desperately needed a "real" job with medical benefits, a retirement plan, and a living wage. I remember, in my imagination, standing before an enormous representation of Society itself, a female figure, books in her arms, pleading to be told what it was I could do to acquire the security and money that until that time, I never felt I needed. "Teach my children!" she said. So I did. In an inner-city barrio high school in the northern San Fernando Valley, California. It was a far cry from the lofty results I had hoped for when I began, but at least it had been on the list of things worth doing.

For sixteen years I served my time in the trenches of the "real" world honestly and to the best of my ability. There with me were six or eight other women, unreformed sixties idealists like me, who had gravitated there the same way I had—as the result of a late but acceptable bargain with society. We knew without asking what to expect from each other. We fought the same battles in unison, treated the students the same loving, respectful way, marched together for the union, agitated against unreasonable authority—all the sixties things. Neither the group of teachers slightly older nor the younger ones, especially, really understood. It was something that couldn't be satisfactorily explained.

Now I am retired and astonished to realize that Lady Society has provided me with a pension. It isn't luxurious, but it is enough for me to gleefully quit being a grown-up and go back to being the pampered child of the sixties that is much more in character. To any person who might suggest I ever again work at some gainful "real world" employment, substitute teaching or at the library or a store, I say, "You've got to be kidding!" For the rest of my life I will never be caught working for money. Instead, I am trying to reconstruct that list of things worth doing. I may even reread Bertrand Russell.

Class Reunion

The invitation from Earlham College, purplish ink on cream-colored paper, arrived in my mailbox not long after I had moved back to Ohio. The event was a special reception and dinner honoring the fortieth reunion of the class of 1961. I had never attended a college reunion. Most years I had lived too far away. This time, however, I couldn't use that excuse, so dressed in long skirt and boots, attire I thought might be appropriately academic, I drove the twenty miles to campus in happy anticipation of an adventure. How often do I get to enter a room full of people forty years older than the last time I saw them?

The campus looked inviting. Earlham stands out like an oasis of serenity between a cemetery and rows of comfortable houses in Richmond, Indiana, a rather battered small city of about 40,000 that presses up awkwardly against the Ohio state line. The campus buildings are tightly clustered in the center of rolling lawns along three sides of a central area known as the Heart. Forty years ago, we were not allowed to walk on the Heart on pain of eternal shunning, but that rule was forsaken some time ago. Behind the Heart is Earlham Hall, formal red brick with white pillars, still the center of campus. Newly added to the rear of Earlham Hall, at least since I attended, is a maze of connected structures housing a theater, art studios, a student Union, and the bookstore.

By the time I got to campus, tired visitors were already leaving for their motels or home after a long day of alumni and parent activities. A group of students had constructed a huge *Peanuts* booth (Lucy's psychiatry stand) where they were selling lemonade along College Avenue. They were sitting in clusters on the lawn or in folding chairs in the relaxed and satisfied afterglow of a term just ended. I remembered being in their posture and looking with curiosity at the alumni from years ago—wondering if that would ever be me. Now it was.

I visited the attractions behind Earlham Hall before heading for the new Athletic and Wellness Center where our gathering was to be held in the Observation Room. It turned out from the Observation Room it was possible to "observe" either the new swimming pool on one side, or on the other, the old gym with bleachers and scoreboard in a building we used to call the field house. Sports were only for jocks in the fifties. Folk dancing was the closest I ever came to exercise, except that required in the mandatory, dreaded Body Mechanics taught energetically by a woman named Bud. Now the Earlham setup rivals Gold's Gym in Los Angeles, complete with refreshment in the food co-op nearby.

The reunion was anticlimactic. I sat with Josie, who had been props mistress for every play I had been in at Earlham, realizing how few dealings I had had with most of the other forty people there. Of course, it made sense when I thought about it. The same people who had organized events on campus, the dorm floor leaders and residence hall committee members, were the ones who would still be organizing such events years later. I had not been in that crowd.

Somewhere between an indifferent performance of a Henry Purcell ditty by the former star of the Earlham Concert Choir and the lengthy appeal for money, Jerry Lemon entertained us with some reminiscences of our time in college. As he talked, I kept picturing him in a beanie, speaking through a megaphone, trying to organize incoming freshmen during orientation. But then, I might have been remembering that other baby-faced guy, Dave, a table away. Neither of them had changed very much. Before the reminiscences, Jerry Lemon recited about twenty age jokes that I had just read on the Internet a few weeks before. The group was quite appreciative not having shared, apparently, the same source, or too polite to notice. Finally, he said something that caught my attention.

"We were still in the innocent age," Jerry Lemon said. "On the cusp. Before the sixties hit." We had been lucky enough to avoid the disruptions and confusion of that time, he felt. He had noticed, however, during the end of his college career, a young man sitting on the lawn with long hair and a guitar and wondered

The Place Just Right

what that was all about. He thought it seemed very strange. "Little did I know what was to come," he concluded.

I thought, "What college did he attend? Surely not the same one I remember."

No wonder I had trouble identifying with these people. They were on the same campus, among the same twelve hundred students, in a little isolated space and time called the late fifties—and they were on another planet. They missed it; apparently, all of it. They were firmly ensconced in the "other generation," the one that was already over thirty at twenty-one and, so it seemed, remained with that generation their entire lives.

They had upon graduation immediately gone on to become doctors, lawyers, church secretaries, and teachers, one of them even a honcho for the Girl Scouts, for God's sake, and they never participated in the glorious, miserable, mind-bending and gut-wrenching cultural and personal revolution in the making. If they had been chewed apart by events, swept away, swallowed, and spit up again by earth-shattering revelations and personal crises as I had been during those years, they showed no signs of it at all. Placid, comfortable, and successful, these representatives of the class of 1961 looked back fondly at convocations, favorite professors, working hard in the cafeteria, and panty raids.

I thought about a scene from *Happy Days* in which the Fonz hits the wrong button on the jukebox and gets Dylan singing "Blowin' in the Wind." He scowls and cringes and later wonders where that stupid song about the weather came from.

As I drove back to Eaton, I realized I had gone to college at a very transitional time and fallen into a circle of friends who were in touch with the first wave of change—who already had a different mind-set about politics, society, sex, and religion. I spent four fervent years accommodating those relationships and ideas with my small-town upbringing. It was a life-changing experience, and it branded me indelibly for decades, still does in ways I am only now fully recognizing.

I used to joke when I was in graduate school that I was bored by my generation, so I wasted a few years and joined the next one. A generation a lot more interesting than my own.

Ajax

In the most serene settings, among the most civilized people, the irrational and primitive will sometimes surface. Like the deeply repressed savagery lurking below the polite demeanor of William Golding's proper schoolboys in *Lord of the Flies*, well-groomed, mannerly students who daily walked the serpentine paths of Earlham College hid impulses not to be imagined in the late fifties on the Old National Trail Road in the rural state of Indiana, American Midwest.

Daniel and John were not boys who attracted attention. They were preppy looking, both dark blond with smooth skin and slight frames. Daniel's face under his crew cut was rounder and sported more freckles; John was shorter of stature and better dressed, but timid and more awkward socially. I knew them both superficially from classes. Some of my friends in the dorm that freshman year knew them better. They were interested in biology and/or anthropology and liked to hang around the museum in the science building.

Life on the first floor of Olvey-Andis dormitory was rife with intrigue, as might be expected in those days, when the doors were locked at 10:00 p.m. and codes of behavior strictly enforced by resident counselors and dorm mothers. Students fell into one of two camps: those who looked for ways to get around the rules and were willing to help others sneak out, smoke, drink, or hide various kinds of contraband; and those who were enforcers or snitches. I fell into the former camp as did, surprisingly, Mary R., from the room at the end of the hall, whose modest grooming, unstylish dress, and naive demeanor screamed Quaker boarding school, but whose heart made no judgments about anyone. She was affectionately known by the unlikely nickname Sullivan. Why, I can't remember, if I ever knew.

The Place Just Right

I first became aware of Daniel and John in a more personal way when several tribal African war spears suddenly appeared in the closet of Sullivan's room. There was much whispering and conjecture, and it quickly became clear these spears were from the collection in the museum. The following events then occurred, I am sure in a rational order, but in my memory of those distant times, they seem to me to have been almost simultaneous: Somebody official came for the spears, and Sullivan and her roommate, a girl most decidedly in the enforcer camp and undoubtedly the snitch, were questioned. Daniel and John and one other young man, whose name might have been Paul, were arrested and incarcerated in the Wayne County, Indiana, jail.

After a day or two, we became aware that while John and Paul had immediately been bailed out and whisked away by wealthy parents, Daniel was still languishing in a jail cell. That was a mighty insult to the sense of justice of several of us, so I, and perhaps somebody else, interceded on his behalf. Dean Curtis, stern and formidable but also sympathetic, saw to it that the young man was sprung, and the next thing I remember is sitting with Daniel on top of a grassy hill near campus while he expressed his gratitude and told me the story.

Earlham College at that time kept a farm just south of the stables, a little beyond the campus. It was customary then for all students to eat, family style, around large round tables in the dining hall, and the produce and livestock raised on the farm helped to supply the menu. Without any impetus from drugs (it was too early for that), but perhaps aided by alcohol, the three boys had stolen the war spears and sneaked down to the farm. Playing around, they entered a barn and began a little ritualistic chanting and pretend war dancing with the spears, centering in, finally, on a pen that contained a nursing sow and her litter. They prodded the sow with the spears; the game got more serious until they were actively stabbing and mutilating the terrified creature and her piglets. The barn became filled with blood and squeals. Once the boys had begun their slaughter, they were unable to stop until it was complete. The sow and her complete litter were dead.

For Daniel it had begun as a game that suddenly and surprisingly turned very intense and out of control. He claimed not to have been the ringleader, and I believed him. He was shaking as he spoke, terrified at what had happened, repelled and fascinated all at the same time. I could hardly make a response. I had grown up around farms, and butchering swine was nothing new, but this was not the same—not the same at all. I was wearing shorts that day; it was late spring. He then told me I had beautiful knees, kissed the one closest to him and left the campus. His college career at Earlham was over.

It was a very hush-hush incident at Earlham College. Hardly anybody was aware it had even happened. The boys simply left early at the end of the year and never came back. It left me wondering how many more such things went on in our idyllic little academic community.

Only seven plays of the Greek genius Sophocles survive in complete form. Most familiar are *Oedipus Rex* and its companion play *Antigone*. Less familiar and almost never produced is an earlier play named for the Greek hero Ajax. During the time of the Trojan War, Ajax becomes enraged when the armor of the fallen hero Achilles is awarded to Odysseus and not to him. In revenge he sets upon the camps of the other Greek soldiers. The goddess Athena intercedes by visiting a fit of madness upon Ajax, causing him instead to slaughter the cattle and other animals kept nearby. When Ajax realizes what he has done, he is humiliated, and after some confusing twists of purpose, kills himself by falling on his sword.

The fifties were a placid time. Young people seemed carefree, innocent, and untroubled by the angst that later came to be associated with growing up. We wore bobby socks, crinoline underskirts, and saddle shoes and looked like the cast of *Pleasantville*. We rocked and rolled and tried to please our parents. But the public face did not always match the private one, and for whatever reasons, some of us didn't make it through those days whole. Many of us didn't make it through those days whole. Conventional fifties society didn't provide for differences and aberrations. It couldn't handle rage and savagery, and when it could not ignore it, hid it away as fast as possible. Athena was kept busy interceding in the cause of order and reason.

I kept in touch with Daniel over the next few years in a sporadic kind of way. Then one night, when we were both in transitional periods of our lives, he called to ask if I would pick him up at the bus station. He needed a place to stay for a while. Incredibly, when I saw him, he was not only scruffy and extremely thin, but he was carrying some drums and other relics from a tribe of natives in New

Guinea. He had spent most of a year with the tribe, presumably on some sort of anthropological research. However, he had lived and slept quite intimately with them, enough to learn that they oiled their bodies with pig grease, he told me with no sense of irony at all.

He stayed a few months—seemed to be settling in. I wasn't ready for that, so we split awkwardly. He accused me of being too conventional and suggested I spend the rest of my life in Lodi, Ohio. I never saw him again.

As for John, the gods in their desire to instruct me arranged that I should learn his fate in a very peculiar manner. Over twenty years later, I found myself filling in for a summer for one of the producers of a theater company in Venice, California. The company was housed in a small city-owned building but wanted to move into a projected new arts center, which was in the planning stages. A reception was held to present a model of the proposed building and to raise money for its construction. The architect was quite well known locally, and we arranged with his office to have the model sent over. It arrived in the hands of two men in white coveralls, workmen I presumed. As they set it up on the display table, I came face-to-face with one of those workmen. It was John, brother of the architect.

I blurted out, "John! It's Brenda, from Earlham College. Do you remember me?"

He rocked back on his heels for a minute, then replied. "I remember you. Nice to see you again." But he got out of there as quickly as possible.

My mind played out in a few seconds a script for his entire life based on the skimpiest of evidence. He was obviously an errand boy for his brother. Had he not ever been on his own? Was he crippled emotionally? Had he possibly repressed that incident for many years? Was it still so painful and embarrassing that he couldn't be in my presence? Or was he some perfectly normal guy just helping out his brother?

I will never know for sure.

Grill Girls and the Sixties

When my best college girlfriend, Carol, finally decided, after decades, to let people know where she was, she announced in the class notes of the *Earlhamite* magazine that she would be interested in hearing from any old friends from the class of 1961, and "especially any of the Grill Girls." I had to laugh. "Grill Girls" was definitely a coded message, its meaning obscure to all but a select few.

Earlham, in those days, was an insane contradiction of values, comprehensible only in light of the fact that we were experiencing the dying days of the fifties and the labor pains of the sixties. School policies combined extreme moral conservatism with an equally extreme political liberalism. On the one hand, strict rules applied for dormitory living including curfews and standards for dress and proper behavior. On the other hand, as a Friends (Quaker) school, Earlham had a traditional sympathy for pacifism, conscientious objection to military service (many of my professors had spent the war confined in camps for pacifists), civil rights reform, and civil disobedience.

The Earlham administration considered censorship and discrimination of any kind intolerable. Any point of view from Nazi to anarchist, communist to atheist, was welcome on campus. But a student could not have a beer in his room, have sex, or even date someone from another race without facing expulsion. For most students these contradictions were neither troubling nor even surprising. However, there were many others who felt the principles of civil disobedience, with which we quickly became familiar in our classes, ought to apply to college rules as well as to unjust federal laws.

As a result, a sizable minority of Earlham students were in various stages of dissatisfaction, disgruntlement, or outright rebellion against college policies in those days, and most of them hung out at the Grill, also known as the Commons—a rather primitive sort of student restaurant in Earlham Hall. Carol and I gravitated there where the cool people lived.

Here were the bridge players and smokers who crammed themselves after dinner into the tiny glass-enclosed smoker's cubicle at the far end of the room, sitting on each other's laps, nestled chest to back, ostracized into intimacy by their cigarettes. Here were the New Yorkers, the Jews, the blacks, and the Young Socialists. Here were the free spirits, the rebels, the confused and messed up, and the displaced urbanites in the alien cornfields of Indiana, homesick and hungry for the closest thing they could find to a public place, laughter, and spirited conversation on our bucolic, isolated campus. For Carol and me that first year, it was a place to escape to from the dorm and from the people there who made us feel naughty and suspect. Later, after Carol was gone, one of the casualties of the contradictions, the Commons became another classroom for me.

From the very first, I was fascinated by the denizens of the Commons, especially the many refugees from New York City and the East who found their way to Earlham expecting the liberalism they were accustomed to and finding, instead, a clash of American cultures as they collided with students from the Midwest. I developed an extremely virulent case of race and culture envy—embarrassed almost to shyness by my bland complexion, my provincialism and obvious cultural deprivation. I was dull and colorless. As far as I could tell, by comparison with them, I had never eaten anything interesting, didn't have a single tradition, dance, or custom to brag about, and had never been anywhere. I was naive, gullible, and ignorant.

It was never a question of my accepting the differences in people in the Commons, but of whether or not they would accept me. I quickly became a smoker, a bridge player, and a Young Socialist. I listened, learned, and persisted, and eventually, they took me in. I got to go places with them, sing with them, feel in touch with something important, and even participate in the first clumsy but fervent protest marches and boycotts in the great metropolis of Richmond, Indiana. My new friends from the East Coast were already involved, by that time, in the early civil rights movement, having cut their teeth singing with the Weavers in summer camps or in clubs back East. In 1960 several of them came back from a conference at Western College in Oxford, Ohio, about thirty miles away. They had had a very inspirational time and incidentally, had learned a new song called "We Shall Overcome."

We were ragtag and simplistic about protests back then. Richmond, Indiana, was not exactly a major target for the civil rights movement nor likely to attract much attention for the cause. Still, we planned our strategy with the local NAACP, whose president ran a barbecue rib place out of the front of his house somewhere in the black section of town. It was the only business in a residential neighborhood. The bathroom was a privy out back. The tables were covered in oilcloth, and the coleslaw was in cheap plastic cups. But the ribs were ambrosia.

I think we must have plotted for months, or maybe my boyfriend, Wally, just liked to take me there for the ribs. The object of the protests was a barber who refused to cut African American hair. The results seem to me to have been ambiguous. As for the boycotts, quite a long list of eating establishments was developed, prominent among them the Blue Note restaurant, one of the few good places to eat in town. Many of the details seem to have receded into the haze of forty years, but I do remember this:

When the weather was warm, we would pile into Wally's old car and head for a quiet spot near the water along Seven Stream Road. Probably that was not the actual name of the road, but the streams were real. They, or perhaps it, ran right across the road, literally—no bridges or dams—seven times. We would count them as we splashed through. We would have brought some beer, food, and a little wine. We would sit on blankets. Somewhere about dusk, the guitars would come out, and we would sing along with the crickets and cicadas. Weavers' songs were an eclectic assortment: Appalachian mountain music, Negro spirituals, international songs, and working songs such as "Erie Canal" or even "Sixteen Tons." Woody Guthrie songs figured prominently.

The singing would start slowly, tentatively, maybe with "Michael Row the Boat Ashore," during which, if you were self-conscious, you could wait for the "hallelujah" and follow the leader. Near the end of the evening it might be "If I Had a Hammer," and it almost always ended with "Goodnight Irene," just like Pete Seeger would have done it. Some of the kids talked about Pete and Lee, Fred or Ronnie, as if they were old friends. The Weavers reportedly talked with their audiences, led them in the songs, got to know the repeaters personally and took an interest in their lives. It seemed less a performance than an extended family reunion. I was jealous I didn't grow up with that. It seems to me that the very early era of folk music, before Peter, Paul and Mary, before even Joan Baez and the Kingston Trio, was much more intimate and personal.

I did get to see Pete Seeger live once, in Cincinnati, where college kids from the entire region gathered for the concert. The beatniks from Antioch College sat in their own section away from the sorority types from Miami of Ohio. Those of us from Earlham looked to be somewhere in the middle. None of that mattered when we all joined in on "Wimoweh." Pete Seeger's reedy tenor soared above us all in that incredible obbligato, and we blended into one wonderful, swaying, uninhibited glob—self-consciousness gone—feeling united in the human race. To me it was intoxicating.

Few critics of the early sixties missed the irony of privileged, middle-class, or white college kids in those years identifying in such numbers and with such dedication with the cause of equal rights. It was more understandable that Jewish or immigrant kids would be in the middle of it. They had at least shared the experience of persecution. To me it was the most natural thing in the world. Like other American young people, I was brought up believing in the American dream and with a strong sense of "justice for all." Once my eyes were opened to the fact that there were whole groups of people who had been excluded from that dream, it was obvious what had to be done. We had to rise up united and change it. The miracle to me was we believed so earnestly we could.

It was truly an age of innocence. Occasionally, usually on PBS, I will stumble across a concert or a television special, which has assembled Peter, Paul and Mary, the Kingston Trio, or some of the other folk groups of that era to perform. It is getting more painful over the years to watch them since they look increasingly more grizzled, old, and anachronistic as they stomp their feet and strum on their guitars, long gray hair pulled back from balding pates in the counterculture ponytail.

I am inclined, when it happens, to turn my back to the screen, hum along and remember. Now and then the cameras will pan the faces of the audience consisting mostly of people, like the performers and me, in various stages of wrinkled, weathered, and gray. It is much easier to watch the audience because they almost all have the same faraway look in their eyes, slightly raised chin and beatific smile. I know they are remembering too. Remembering how it felt to be so young, so filled with purpose, and so confident we could change the world.

I didn't feel like a conjurer. Although the night was late and the moon full, neither a cauldron nor Graymalkin was in sight. Just me in my self-made cubicle in front of the computer, idly moving the cursor and my mind through a senseless game. I was looking for distraction, actually, not a voice from the past. Dotty, my mother-in-law, was perhaps on her deathbed in New York, and any ring of the phone had sent me lunging for the receiver, my heart in my throat, all day long.

The phone rang.

"Hello!"

"Brenda?"

"Yes."

"It's Wally. I just got back from Mexico, and tonight your letter fell out of some mail I had stacked here."

Months ago, shortly before Christmas, I had gone through my address book and sent one of those "We've Moved!" cards, the kind with the cute picket fence and welcome mat, to everyone listed whether I had been in touch recently or not. Some people, like Wally, I had not talked to in twenty years. I figured it was time to stop kidding myself and bite the bullet. If I got an answer, that meant they still remembered; if not, then I would paste over the name and write in my local air-conditioning repairman or someone more likely to be important in my new life. I had been a terrible correspondent while living in Los Angeles and allowed relationships, even those once terribly important to me, to die of neglect. I felt compelled to cut my losses. There were several painful ones that made me cringe as I pasted over them: Carol, Rosalind, Thom—and Wally. Hecate still lives. Here he was.

We caught up.

His ex-wife had moved back to the island off Washington State where they had bought land decades ago. When they divorced, Wally had promised her the

The Place Just Right

house whenever she wanted, and after twenty-two years, she had taken him up on it. He moved into a one-room cabin. His married daughter lived nearby, his son also, a grandchild on the way. They had a kind of compound where even the dogs, chickens, and sheep all seemed to get along. It was mellow. He was semiretired and spent his time on boats, sailing and working. For three months of the year he lived in Baja, California. He was proud they had gotten Jet Skis outlawed in the area, and he heated his cabin with solar heat. He was a modern-day Luddite, with no computer or other electrical devices—living simply, incurring minimal expenses. I smiled as I listened. If any one of us was destined to live past the sixties uncorrupted, it would have had to have been Wally. Not an iota of materialism, mainstream ambition, or complexity was detectable as we spoke.

"You won't believe this," I said, "but you have been on my mind a lot lately. I have been writing a sort-of memoir, and my mind has been full of those days."

"I'm not surprised. These things have happened to me before."

I peppered him with questions. Where were we going on Seven Stream Road? (Blue Clay Falls, southeast of town, but he remembered hunting for fossils more than the singing.) What was the name of the NAACP guy he worked with? (He didn't know but remembered that his wife had been very proper.) Whatever happened to the barber who refused to cut the hair of African Americans? (He didn't remember, but by that time he was more involved in some plan to find people jobs.) I got a little more personal.

"Wally, were you really mad at me about the Blue Note Restaurant?"

"What do you mean?"

"I ate there with my roommate, remember? It was boycotted. I thought you were really upset."

"It was no big deal. I ate there sometimes, too."

"I thought it broke us up."

"No, don't you remember? We were together after that."

Suddenly, I did remember. A carriage house on Long Island after I came back from my senior semester abroad. The way his thick, black hair fell over his forehead, the line it made against his neck. His smooth, hairless chest; his compact body, muscular and graceful. And his wonderful hands, skillful and competent;

shuffling cards with a flourish, moving along the guitar, tinkering with the old car, unbuttoning my blouse.

"Are you still skinny?" he asked.

"I put on a lot of weight after an operation," I said. "But I've been losing it again. I'm down to a hundred and forty pounds. How about you? Did you get fat?"

"Not really," he said. "About one fifty-five. Are you aging well?"

"I don't have too many wrinkles. But I'm starting to droop around the chin. It doesn't matter," I answered. "I never got along on my looks anyway."

"That wasn't what I thought."

"You never said anything."

"I was terrible at expressing my feelings."

"And I always presumed the worst."

There it was. After forty years, I understood.

"We played a lot of kissy face, didn't we?" he said.

For a moment I knew that if I could see to the end of the phone line, there he would be. Twenty-one years old, grinning, naughty and beautiful. I was grinning, too, terribly grateful he couldn't see my smile, or the flush coming up in my cheeks. Grateful he couldn't hear me catch my breath.

"Yes, we did," I replied. "But it was a long time ago."

"A long time ago." he repeated.

We said goodbye and promised to keep in touch more often than once every twenty years.

Dotty made it through the night.

Senioritis

There is probably a good reason that the "semester abroad" is usually in the junior year of college. To the young, unsophisticated and naive, experiencing a foreign culture is such a shock it requires a full year back in the "normalcy" of college life to recover before the next major crossroad appears—graduation. Impulsively, I went to Italy my senior year instead of the usual junior year and, immediately upon my return to campus, was thrust into the first real depression of my life. Senioritis in spades—desolation, confusion, intense anger and rebellion, and indecision bordering on despair. I had no idea what was happening to me. The feelings were new, unanticipated, and totally uncharacteristic. I cried much of the time for a couple of months, and when I wasn't crying, I was hateful or manic.

I shouldn't even have been in college. I had all my credits already, but I stayed to play Cleopatra in the spring production of *Antony and Cleopatra*. I could barely go about a daily routine. I even flunked a class outright—American Literature, which I was taking for no particular reason anyway. The class had thrust me backward into the same frame of mind I had had in early high school when, because of a problem with "authority," or maybe just plain obnoxiousness, I spent many hours in the principal's office and humiliated my mother.

I hated the American Lit professor. She was a colorless, stout, self-important prude, in my estimation. No matter she was an icon at the college, beloved by all the English majors. That only made me hate her more. I hated English majors, all of them. There were a batch of them at the house I lived in. I called them the Sunshine Girls for their super soft-spoken optimism and maudlin intensity about poetry. I despised poetry, except for Shakespeare, of course, which was different. Besides, with their Eastern boarding-school backgrounds and establishment correctness, I just knew none of them approved of me. I would come into the house late, after rehearsal, and there they would be—hunched over the study table, comfortable in their curlers and chenille bathrobes, looking up at me from their thick books and term papers. It was all I could do to be civil.

I was often on the very edge of civility in those days. My mind would seize on some irritating scheme to rattle the judgmental people all around—a sarcastic comment or dirty trick. Then common decency would prevail, and I would be forced to squelch the impulse, never easy for me. It was a constant battle with the urge to flout authority. Sometimes it would just break out, although never directly at anyone—more obliquely. I would bang out something loud on the piano in the house at odd hours, or cut up at a dorm meeting. Once my new boyfriend and I smashed a bowl of Christmas ornaments against the fireplace one by one and watched the colored glass shatter. I still remember vividly the confused, pained look the housemother gave me when she saw the mess. She didn't understand what could have possessed us to do that. Nor could I.

Somehow the days crept by, and the term and my college career reached their shaky end. Having made no plans for anything, I returned home to Eaton and took a job teaching in one of the village high schools in the county. It was a bad idea. Not only was I totally unprepared to be teaching anybody anything, I had returned to my mother's house and, naturally, continued my rebellion by fighting with her. This lasted until I put an end to this part of my life by impulsively eloping to North Carolina with my nineteen-year-old New Yorker boyfriend, Tom.

Riding the Freeway

In 1963, towing a twenty-four-foot travel trailer, I naively pulled onto a freeway in San Diego, having just arrived from Ohio. The confusion of merging with that chaotic ribbon of speeding cars and trucks caused not only the trailer, but also my equilibrium, to weave like a drunken San Diego sailor. I was sure I was going to die. It only got worse when I went by my exit twice in both directions before I had positioned myself to get off that damn road at the correct place, the little piece of paper on which I had scribbled my directions trying to blow right off the dashboard. I remember this clearly because it seems now the perfect metaphor for my life in the sixties. For many lives, I think.

Once, back in Eaton, on a break from college, I ran into a pregnant high-school classmate pushing a shopping cart loaded with groceries and babies. "Ain't you married yit?" she said to me. I saw her again last year at one of our class reunions. She never left Preble County. Her husband delivers propane gas; in fact, twice a year, he now delivers my propane gas for cooking. The speeding highway that symbolized the unsettled life of the sixties was something she had only watched on television.

Some young people, like the prodigal son, have always left home to seek their fortunes, just as other young people have stayed put. Both are fine American traditions. But in the sixties the wanderers captured the most attention, more of us moving further from our roots than in previous generations, not only physically, but culturally as well. I am sure cultural historians have good explanations for this movement, but back then, for me, it was very simple. I would not have decided on my own to go anywhere. Like most girls, I was never encouraged to think in terms of goals or careers. Totally unencumbered by any particular ambition or purpose, I was, therefore, pushed and pulled by whatever errant winds blew my way. In 1963 those winds were marriage and the military.

As my mother sensed, the nineteen-year-old boy I impulsively married in 1961 was even less focused than I was. Restless in college after two years and looking for something more immediately gratifying, he abruptly joined the United States Coast Guard. He hadn't been in boot camp two weeks before I received a phone call from him saying, "Call my mother. Have her hire a lawyer and get me out of here!" That proved impossible. He was stuck. At least until a fortuitous blow on the head from a drawbridge gate in New Orleans, less than a year later, gave him and the military an excuse for a discharge. I don't quite remember how; it was all very murky, even then.

However bizarre, this series of events was the windstorm that uprooted me from the Midwest and set me on a very different path from my classmate married to the propane gas deliverer. Instead of pushing children in a grocery cart in Eaton, Ohio, I ironed sailor suits in a tiny trailer court nestled under an overpass in San Diego, making desultory stabs at cooking and housekeeping, and driving back and forth to the base under the palm trees of California to the tune of "Dominique" by the Singing Nun. I didn't even try to get a job until we were transferred to New Orleans.

In New Orleans we obtained a better, larger trailer, a step up, to tell the truth, from the dilapidated housing of many of the other Coast Guard families who were stationed at the base on Lake Pontchartrain. I will always associate the sixties with aging houses and cheap apartments, with stained wooden floors under fraying carpet, chipped linoleum, sagging porch steps, and graying paint. I came to live in several such places as the decade progressed.

These houses were comfortable and friendly, but never really home. Like old broads, they bore the scars of previous encounters: layers of paint that if scraped with a putty knife revealed the color preferences of several previous tenants, mysterious scratches or dents in the walls or woodwork suggesting scuffles or accidents. Sometimes objects were discovered in corners of closets or under sinks: marbles, perhaps, or forks and spoons, pieces of broken glass or plastic toys, hairpins and paper clips, each bearing witness to the succession of people who had previously laid claim to the space. We were a transient subculture in temporary shelter, setting up and taking down our concrete block and board shelving on or from the nearest wall. The fine arts of homemaking became unimportant. What was the use? Next year we would be someplace else.

It was in New Orleans in the fall and winter of 1963 when I began to notice the world was different. I didn't know whether the times were a-changin' or if I had simply been thrust into a very strange place. The impressions began when I went to an agency for help in finding employment. An extremely enthusiastic woman with a "Nawlins" accent that positively sang out loud took me on with relish. My first stop was a "gutsy little publisher" that she obviously admired to death. It turned out to be the John Birch Society, located in one of the many seedy but fascinating areas of the city. I took one look at the pamphlets at the John Birch Society claiming Nelson Rockefeller was a communist, and Dwight Eisenhower a man who betrayed the true America, and said, "No, thank you."

I wasn't any more enthralled with the secretarial job at the district attorney's office. I was interviewed by the now infamous Jim Garrison himself, who was brusque and indifferent. As I waited in his office, I could see his desk was littered with police reports of the most lurid sort—pictures of bruised and bloody victims of some assault or other, and a graphic description of the activities of two homosexuals in a car as viewed by the arresting officer. Had I been hired, I might have had an insider's view of the historic events about to transpire surrounding the Kennedy assassination. It was not to be.

Finally, in exasperation, my employment adviser found the perfect solution—English teacher at St. Dominic parish school near Lake Pontchartrain. I wasn't thrilled to be teaching again so soon, but the children were orderly. They had to be. They began their day kneeling to kiss the ring of Mother Mary James as she moved about the play yard, less than five feet tall and elegant in her habit and wimple. They started each class standing at their desks until I gave them permission to be seated. The curriculum was heavy on grammar, writing, and sentence diagramming, with which, thanks to my mother's example, I was comfortable.

It was in the orderly and reverent atmosphere of St. Dominic school that I experienced the day of the assassination of President Kennedy, shepherding with me to the chapel a frightened little girl named Shirley, the only Protestant in the school, who was as confused by the Catholic ritual almost as much as by the events of that historic day.

It was only a short time later, after my Coast Guardsman had attempted to outrun a dinging opening drawbridge gate on his motor scooter and been struck in the head, after the hasty and premature discharge, that we left New Orleans and military life for good. On the night before we left, I stood in the doorway of a shabby second-story apartment of another Coast Guard family watching the Beatles' first appearance on *The Ed Sullivan Show*. We had stopped to say goodbye and paused to watch the musicians who had been creating such interest. It was clear to me that the day Kennedy was shot would go down in history. It was not clear that the particular television moment I was watching would, in its own way, change the world as much.

My young husband and I headed back to the Midwest—back to Longer's Trailer Court on the sterile eastern edge of Richmond, Indiana, among the fast-food restaurants, auto dealerships, and motels. Mostly, however, we returned to the reality of a disintegrating marriage, to infidelity and recrimination, to betrayal, pain, and the inevitable divorce my mother had foreseen. The chaotic ride that had lurched and sped its way into San Diego, and jerked and swerved through New Orleans, deposited me back exactly where I began, only this time at a crossroads. For the first time in my life, I did not wait for the next errant wind. Instead, I made a bold decision. I would immerse myself in the only world I had ever found that could promise, unequivocally, comfort, nurturing, and refuge—the theater.

Theater

Playing Kate in *Taming of the Shrew* at Earlham College.

Rosalie Kramer Unger, my loyal high-school classmate who introduced me to the Alpha Garden Club, has also invited me to join a Saturday morning breakfast group. Five of us meet at the Eaton Place for companionship, gossip, and a few laughs. One of our members, Joanne, a local history buff, recently brought in clippings from a 1955 *Register-Herald* she had found while researching for the upcoming Preble County Bicentennial. She handed me a short article and picture announcing the cast for a high-school production of *Drums of*

Death. Rosalie and I were in the front row. We tried very hard without success to remember what the play was about. I had a misty vision of myself weaving over a fake bonfire in the middle of the stage casting some sort of spell. Rosalie remembered nothing at all.

I had an acting teacher in Minnesota who teased us once by saying as actors we were pretentious to consider ourselves artists. We were, in actuality, he said, just a bunch of people who needed a lot of attention. There is more than a shred of truth in that. When Rosalie and I were in high school, being "in plays" and going to "play practice" was, at first, just another activity. I learned very quickly, however, that it brought me much gratifying admiration and praise, quite enough in those years to recommend it. I was neither a cheerleader nor a baton twirler like Betty Jane, and I wasn't terribly popular with the boys, so I learned to love acting instead—being onstage, feeling the audience respond, hearing applause. It was my own moment of glory.

It worked just as well when I tried it at college. Not only did performing give me an identity on my small campus, endearing me to people who might otherwise have raised their eyebrows at some of my rebellions, it also became the principal instrument of my education and personal growth, introducing me to the mysteries of my own creativity and to the wonders of Shaw, Shakespeare, Sophocles, and a whole host of other artists and writers. Since much of the great literature of the world is expressed in dramatic form, this meant I received a wide-ranging classical education—a realization I didn't put together until many years later. Of course, I had help. Help from an inspired teacher with the ability to turn my hunger for attention into a twenty-five-year obsession with the theater in all its forms.

My first memory of Arthur Little is of a bearded, puckish middle-aged man showing a little boy how to act like a child. The play was William Saroyan's *My Heart's in the Highlands*, and part of the set was a porch railing standing out darkly against a rose-colored cyclorama. It was a late, perhaps technical rehearsal, and the play had stopped because the moment was not yet right. People were standing around watching as Arthur draped himself over the railing like a monkey on a jungle gym. He somersaulted over it, peered mischievously through the open spaces, splayed out on the porch, and reached around the posts after imaginary insects. He sat on it and dangled his feet as if it were a dock in the water. It was possible to see the running stream, a fishing hat and pole on the empty stage beside him.

Arthur Little

I had been in plays in high school. I had postured and declaimed and been congratulated, but nobody had ever shown me what acting really was. In that moment I got a glimpse, enough to keep me enthralled for most of my life. I took to the theater like an iron filing to a magnet. It became my work, my recreation, and my motivation. And Arthur Little, for a time at least, became my inspiration.

As a teacher, Arthur Little was the genuine article. He was already legendary at Earlham College by the time I came under his influence. They called him the "Bohemian Quaker" and lavished love and appreciation on him, everything except enough money to make a real theater department. He used to say sadly, "If I only had a colleague." The fine arts were still rather suspect as a valid part of the traditional academic curriculum, and Earlham was conservative in that regard. It was impossible, in fact, to be a drama major. It had to be paired with something else. Nevertheless, Arthur Little adored Shakespeare, George Bernard Shaw, Stanislavski, and his job.

Sara Little, his patient wife, told me once that Arthur regularly "fell in love" with a student. There was nothing amiss about it. He simply became enraptured with the mind and talent of one of his students and focused on that person, male or female, with every fiber of his mentoring skills. I was that lucky student. Surely, I was not the only one during that time, but I believed I was, and that made all the difference. I felt his concern, his interest, and his love constantly.

Arthur had a philosophy of teaching that must have come from the unlikely pairing of his Quaker beliefs and his understanding of the art of acting, a quite improbable combination, but incredibly effective in its application. He used to say that while the Quakers believed a part of God was in every person, Stanislavski believed that there was that of every person in every other person. The trick as an actor was to call it up in you. So he headed directly for whatever resided deep inside—helping his actors search for experiences, secrets, hopes, desires, pain, and sadness—whatever was needed to create a character or a moment onstage. He loved the paradox of the actor who while grieving, perhaps, over the death of a loved one, or falling in love, would feel compelled at the same time to stop and register the emotions for future use in his craft.

None of this is a revelation to anyone who has ever been a theater student. Anyone in theater has to be, in fact, a perpetual student. The acting coach and actor relationship is possibly one of the most intimate of any that is not personal. Imagine the actor onstage in rehearsal digging inside for a tone of feeling, for tears or laughter, searching for an inflection, a meaningful pause. Then imagine, at just the right moment, the intervention of the voice from the empty theater, the face at the edge of the stage, the quiet conference as the actor leans down to hear an instruction—that is a wonderful thing. It means that in a very personal struggle for expression and understanding, someone has been through it with you, breath by breath, and knows better than you do where the struggle is leading and how to complete the creative act. This, in my opinion, is the pinnacle of teaching. The brilliant lecture, the seminar, the corrected paper, all pale by comparison. And no face at the edge of the stage was more comforting, more confidence inspiring than the bearded visage of Arthur Little. I trusted him absolutely.

About ten years after I left Earlham, a reunion was held for theater students, and a revival of an act from one of Arthur's favorite plays, *The Skin of our Teeth* by Thornton Wilder, was planned. I was allowed to play Sabina for that revival, but only after I promised Arthur that I hadn't gotten fat and still looked good in the little French maid outfit she wore. I was in graduate school at the time and came down for the rehearsal and performance. It was a thrown-together sort of thing. At one moment during the monologue, I walked to the edge of the stage and asked Arthur a question about the timing of a line. The bearded visage looked up quizzically and smiled. "Don't you know?" he said. "You know more about that now than I do." I was flabbergasted. With a total absence of ego and with pride in his voice, he had just cut the cord and set me free. It was the ultimate gift from a teacher to a student. Graduation.

The last time I saw Arthur my husband, Jon, and I were on our way to California. We stopped in with our son, then not quite two years old, for a visit. After a little while, our baby got fussy, and Arthur went into the kitchen and returned with a wooden spoon. Before he handed it to our little boy, he showed him how to play with it. It became a drumstick, a walking cane, a hairbrush, a baseball bat, an ice cream cone…

I was told, by whom I don't remember, that when Arthur learned he had prostate cancer and not much longer to live, he said the following, or something akin to it: "It is not enough to accept this; I have to will it to happen." This could be another part of the legend, but I would not be surprised if it's true. Arthur knew that in life, as in theater, when the moment is not right, you have to stop the show and fix it. Even if it is in a late rehearsal. No matter what script the actor is handed, the key to success is always in the motivation. Stanislavski would have been proud.

As for me, I am still leaning down at the edge of the stage to hear the whispered suggestions of the "Bohemian Quaker." They are imaginary now, but no less real to me for all that. After all, imagination is what theater is about. Arthur would understand. Absolutely.

Jumping In

Just inside the gated entrance to Lakengren, at the second road to the right, an arrow points to the swimming pool. The pool itself, small by California standards but generous for Ohio, sits with picnic tables, playground equipment, and adjoining service buildings on a small hill surrounded on all sides by gravel roads and modest houses. Since the board of directors has never invested the money to heat it, the swimming season is short, Memorial Day to Labor Day. Nevertheless, during the summer, the Lakengren Women's Club offers a class in aerobic water exercise, which, happily, I have joined. I grew up a water rat on the beach at Lake Erie and, to this day, find total immersion in water the best therapy imaginable. I suppose the group, mostly retirees, could be called borderline geriatric. However, the ladies are pretty spry. It takes a youthful spirit to brave that frigid water on days following a rain or a cold spell.

Today, Virginia and I weren't really late for water exercise at the Lakengren pool; it just felt that way. Shirley, our current volunteer leader, always starts on the dot of eleven, ready or not. Shirley doesn't mean to rush us; she just moves faster than most people. Her internal engine seems to be calibrated differently. She was already past the twist and into cross-country as Virginia descended the ladder into the middle of the pool, and I walked around the edge to hit the steps. It was then I saw a large brown mouse swimming desperately around the perimeter of the pool, tiny feet almost invisible as they frantically churned the water. "Oh, my God," I said, something short of an *eek*. "There's a mouse in the pool." It created a sensation.

The screaming and laughing continued until our lifeguard, Kara, under the confusing and energetic advice of everyone else (from a safe distance), and after

The Place Just Right

several extremely squeamish false starts, managed to net the mouse out of a drain and send it scampering into the bushes along the side of the pool house. The incident made my day, giving me something to chuckle about for most of the afternoon. These days, in the quiet of retirement and the isolation of the country, I relish whatever entertainment comes along.

Truth to tell, however, jumping into the pool with the ladies has had more than entertainment value. It has been a daily educational video on the subject of a new way of life for me: life as a woman growing older, and life as a relative newcomer trying to make her way again in the now unfamiliar Midwest. I watch, I absorb, and I am often amazed at what I see and hear.

"I would love to go to the barbecue at the beach," she said, plaintively, between punches and jumping jacks. "But I'm not sure *he'll* let me. So far I can't get him to say."

Moving up and down in knee bends at the side of the pool, I swallowed my shock and tried to remember that she probably married, as did I the first time, at least ten years before the women's movement and remained in the generation of couples still unaffected by that particular revolution.

As we bicycled forward and back, two minutes each way, we shared our lives, and I felt in this group of women genuine concern and support, each for the other. Support for the lady who is spending exhausting hours every day waiting hand and foot on an invalid mother-in-law. Concern for knee and hip surgeries, for what the doctor might say at the husband's next visit, for grandchildren in trouble and neighbors getting too old to manage anymore. One day we spontaneously grabbed hands and prayed for our friend who had lost a grandchild to diabetes through some tragic and unnecessary error, all of us meeting later to visit the funeral home in a nearby small village and witness long, sad lines of Little League teams in uniform and other schoolchildren winding around the block.

There are happier kinds of sharing, too. While getting out the milk jugs for crunches and the scissors, we hear about vacations, visits from children and grandchildren, even about motorcycling excursions from one of our more adventurous members.

Maybe it's the cooling softness of the water, or possibly the warm breeze that sometimes arrives from nowhere to ripple the blue surface and Virginia's silver hair. It might be the killdeer calling out in flight, or the crunch of tires on gravel as the security truck pulls into the parking area. Surely the laughter of children playing across the street and the panorama of white clouds against the summer sky contribute. Or possibly it is just the companionship of women who understand each other, are inclined by nature and experience to trust each other, and instinctively know that as surely as their bodies need the exercise, their souls need to share the events of their lives, however casually and haltingly they are told. Whatever it is, there are days at the pool that feel for all the world as cozy as family sharing a winter evening before a fireplace. I have, it seems, jumped into more than just water when I opted to join the ladies at the pool.

"This has been a wonderful class this summer!" Shirley says. "I hate to see it end!" We all agree.

Because her internal engine is calibrated just a little differently, making her move faster than most people, Shirley usually finishes five to ten minutes before the prescribed hour of twelve o'clock. It is time for each of us to spend as we wish before they open the pool to the children waiting impatiently outside the chain-link fence. During this time, I like nothing better than to leave my glasses safely at the edge of the pool and swim—swim the way I used to when I was a water rat growing up along the shores of Lake Erie.

Water has an incredibly miraculous ability to erase age or infirmity for the person floating in it. It is appropriate that the legendary search for youth ends at a fountain. The mistake is to believe the water is for drinking. The trick is to plunge in. Most of my fellow class members at the Lakengren pool, never swimmers to begin with, don't understand. They never learned to trust the security of immersion in water in the first place, and they are too fearful now to learn the secret.

I was never a natural athlete like my mother, never perspired through regular workouts as many do to fight off aging and stay fit. I have a hip that hurts after an hour or so on my feet and knees that are sensitive to jolting. My days of running around the block are over, and I will not now try a back bend, cartwheel,

The Place Just Right

or even a somersault without miles of mats. But I will cannonball off the edge of the pool, grab my knees and somersault under water, dive to the bottom of the pool to retrieve whatever fell there, and swim under the surface without a breath almost as far as I used to. No gravity to fight, no aches, no insecurity, no fear.

Sometimes, in the five or ten minutes Shirley leaves us after class, I float on my back in the deep end of the pool and slowly rotate under water backward in a long circle, as Esther Williams used to do in her movies. Esther Williams was my idol. My friend Molly and I called that particular move the Catalina. When I do it now, I am still fourteen. My body feels slim; my tanned legs, glimpsed just under the sunlit surface of the pool, firm and smooth. It is a luxurious indulgence in vanity and sensuousness for a woman in retirement—one I am determined to make for many, many years to come.

⁓

When the pool closed in September, Shirley and I, reluctant to have the exercise end, signed up for a more professionally organized water exercise class at Miami University. Twice a week we got up at dawn to speed sixteen miles along country roads, through tiny Sugar Valley and even smaller Morning Sun, my all-time favorite name for a village, past Hueston Woods State Park to Oxford, Ohio, passing much of the same forested scenery I saw so long ago when, taking control of my own life, I drove to Miami every day as a graduate student in theater. I never would have believed, after I left Miami the first time, that I would ever in my life be making that trip again, and for a reason somewhat similar—to immerse myself in an activity designed to cure whatever ailed me. It seemed to me my life was recycling.

College towns are soothing places, and Oxford is no exception. The town itself is still dominated by vine-covered brick buildings, shady streets with old frame houses converted to student housing, and a long thoroughfare in the middle, lined with college shops, restaurants, and watering holes. In those days I saw little of the town, however, since I was swallowed up in Fisher Hall, the old but comfortable building that housed the theater complex. Immersion indeed.

Every day was exhaustingly full of classes in theater history, literature, or performance. Every evening stretched late in rehearsal. I acted; I wrote and produced a play; I directed *Arms and the Man* by Shaw for the summer theater; I costumed a production of *The Merchant of Venice*; I worked in the shop building sets and in the office publicizing the plays and selling tickets. I bonded with my teachers and befriended my fellow students, and by the end of it, a subtle but significant change had occurred. I was no longer a graduate student; I now considered myself a "theater person."

About ten years after leaving Miami, I heard for the first time the old joke about the circus performer who had fallen on hard times with his act and was reduced to following the elephants around with a shovel cleaning up their excrement. An old friend from the performer's youth took pity on him and offered him a well-paying job in commerce. The performer immediately refused. "What?" he said indignantly. "And leave show business?"

I found the joke hilarious at the time, although on more than one occasion in the years that followed, the humor became a little strained. Every theater teacher I had, at whatever level, felt obligated to deliver a lecture to his or her students that said in essence: "Your chances of success in the theater are minuscule. You need to know the odds are totally against you no matter how talented you are. For the sake of your future and that of your family, you must think long and hard about the obstacles you face, the rejection, the humiliation, and the years you will spend paying dues. I heartily discourage you from going into this field!" It is hard to imagine a teacher in any other subject, math, for instance, or business, feeling compelled to deliver such a talk. Only in the arts.

Usually that lecture discouraged no one. It only underscored the obvious truth. The way to succeed in theater is to be more determined, or lucky, than the rest of the pack. Most theater people, if they believe in nothing else, believe in themselves and their own determination. Besides, the theater is addicting. The creative struggle, the thrill of success, basking in the approval of an audience, and the wonderful, funny, clever people, larger than life, are all huge and immediate satisfactions. Once in, it is very difficult to ever imagine living any other way.

The Place Just Right

So I stayed in theater as long as I could. For about twelve years, staying in theater for me meant staying in college as a student or teacher, sometimes both at the same time. The educational theater was a welcome source of income and a comfortable creative home. It took me first to a job at what was then Wisconsin State University—Oshkosh then to graduate school in Minneapolis, and finally, with my husband, Jon, to North Carolina. After that, I got to be a part of the professional theater world in Los Angeles, where I would have happily spent the rest of my working years, had life not intervened to pull me away.

Peter Pan

I came awake slowly in Linda's sofa bed in her den on a sun-dotted Sunday morning in fragrant Alhambra, California. I had been running all week, catching up with this person and that, cramming as much as I could into my first trip back to California since moving away almost three years before. I was tired but feeling good. People still remembered me, were going out of their way to spend time with me. I took a few extra minutes to curl up and relive it before going out to join Linda and Bettie for breakfast. I could hear them laughing in the kitchen. It was Bettie's first time back, too, since she moved to Atlanta. There was a lot to share.

When I finally shuffled into the kitchen, the coffee was made and the bagels toasted, and wonder of wonders, a *Sunday Los Angeles Times* lay scattered out on the table in the breakfast nook. Bettie was already waiting for me impatiently, pencil poised over the crossword puzzle. It was a treat as delicious as dipping strawberries in chocolate—an actual *L.A. Times* crossword and someone to do it with. We used to bring them to school on Monday mornings, get in a huddle during nutrition break and/or lunch to figure out the hard ones we had struggled with by ourselves. My best teacher buddies. All week I had been realizing how much I missed them. It's just not the same on the phone.

We dispatched the puzzle rather efficiently, I thought, and I idly picked up the Calendar section of the paper. I got to the second page. "Well," I announced. "There's a guy I've been to bed with."

I watched the reaction, and they didn't miss a beat. "I swear," said Linda, with just the right amount of exasperation in her voice, "you can't even show her a newspaper!"

The Place Just Right

"Why you little sl-ut." This from Bettie in her best Atlanta drawl, grinning just as wide as she could. I knew they would love it. The best part was that it was the truth. And they knew it.

"So tell us. What's the story with that?"

"Well, actually," I hemmed and hawed, making the thing a whole lot worse. "With this guy it was just one time, one of those 'friends helping friends' things. You know." Linda nodded. She did know.

Bettie looked at both of us vacantly. "If you say so." she said, innocently.

"The real story was his partner."

I could see it was getting too complicated to get into on a sun-dotted Sunday morning in fragrant Alhambra, California. So we didn't. There was too much else current to catch up on. But later, on the long, lonely plane ride back to Ohio, I thought about it again, long and hard.

They were a comedy team that used to play the college circuit back when they themselves had just graduated, and I was getting ready to leave Wisconsin for Minnesota. The article in the *L.A. Times* was a feature on an annual convention held for people who booked entertainment for the colleges. My "friend" whose name jumped out at me from the newspaper had apparently become a honcho for the bookers. He was quoted frequently concerning the sorts of acts likely to have the most success with college audiences. There was no mention of his former partner. The last I knew, he was married and living in Midtown Manhattan on the West Side, still doing stand-up comedy in clubs. My last communication, when I moved to Ohio, had been returned, address unknown. I had felt the tug of a loss. Our contact over the past decades had been sporadic at best, an occasional card or short meeting in New York, but at least I felt I knew where he was. Now I can only imagine.

I first met both of them when my housemate, Patti, agreed to help them with their developing act. Patti was a new Ph.D., a recently hired professor in the Theater Department at Wisconsin with two little girls to raise by herself. She considered her specialty to be directing, but she would have made a fabulous lounge singer. Her rendition of George Gershwin's "Do It Again" at the piano made me green with envy. I could act up a storm, but singing was my Achilles' heel. My voice and I would both seize up, and I was never sure which was to blame.

Patti was no intellectual snob, quite the contrary. She loved popular entertainment and made it her business to scout clubs and keep up with the local talent. She took the new comedy team under her wing. I suppose you could say she had adopted me also, in a different way. She suggested we live together. It helped me keep active in theater activities since I was teaching, principally, speech and debate, and I could help her with the girls.

To this day I couldn't say how the new stand-up comedian and I got from two people both hanging around Patti's house to an "involvement," if you could call it that. It was not only unlikely; it was preposterous. He wasn't that much younger than I, probably four or five years, very tall, broad-shouldered, Irish with freckles and a playful face. Still, he was about the last man in the world I thought I would have been attracted to. I yearned for serious, sensitive men. He was a life-of-the-party sort of guy— outrageous and wildly funny. He had been famous on campus for raunchy fraternity pranks and for delivering a hysterically funny speech at commencement in fake Latin, some felt trashing the whole ceremony.

His routine onstage, beyond the banter and skits with his partner, consisted largely of sound effects: loud, rhythmic sound effects achieved by cozying up to the microphone and letting go with the din of an aerial dogfight in World War I or the whines from a high-speed auto race. When he really got it going, it had the effect of a drum solo in a good jazz combo, a postmodern improvisation on the subject of noise. It was a highly evolved version of a little boy with two Matchbox cars play-crashing them together over and over. Bam. Bam. Bam!!! A child in a man's body.

I think it began out of nowhere one day when he simply took me by the hand, led me out of the house, and said. "Come on. We're going to go out and play." We went out by the lake among some grassy dunes and chased each other around until after dark in some sort of pretend war maneuvers, like the Lost Boys in Neverland stalking the Indians. It was sort of fun, except I dropped one of his knives and almost lost it in the darkness. He forgave me. Then we went back to his place, and he took my hand again, led me upstairs, and said. "Now we're going to see the sun come up." That was the most glorious sunrise I ever remember.

The Place Just Right

There is a scene in *The Last Picture Show* in which Ellen Burstyn, playing a frustrated, unhappy housewife and mother, says about the man with whom she was reputed to have had an affair, "If it hadn't been for him, I wouldn't have known what 'it' was." I never took that to mean love. I took that to mean sexual chemistry, and in that sense, I feel the same way about the stand-up comedian. It was a classic case of knowing this was not a man to even think about marrying, but wanting him anyway.

In fact, I never had even the slimmest chance of developing any illusions about our "relationship." It was shortly after another encounter, after a sweaty, athletic night that ended with a wild careening ride to Chicago, so I could arrive disheveled and out of breath to judge an early-morning debate tournament, I realized he was also sleeping with Patti! She was none too pleased with either one of us and had no inhibitions about letting us know it.

"I asked you," I yelled. "I asked you straight out if there was anything going on between you and Patti. And you told me, 'No.'"

"I lied," he said, sheepishly.

We cooled it. Except for the middle of one night at the house when he tap-tapped on my bedroom door, like Peter Pan at Wendy's window, sneaked in, and crawled into my bed.

"You can't do this!" I whispered as loud as I dared.

"Watch me." he whispered back.

I might have kicked him totally out of my life, in exasperation, if nothing else, if it hadn't been for what he did on Christmas Day that year. Patti took the kids to her parents for the holidays, but for the first time in my entire life, I had nowhere to go. My mother was on an Airstream Travel Trailer Caravan to Central America with my stepfather, and my beloved grandmother, with whom my fondest Christmases had been spent, had passed away. Patti and the girls asked me along, but I was too sad to put up some front with strangers. "I'll be just fine," I promised. "I plan to curl up in front of the fire with a good book and relax, for a change."

I really thought it would be fine, and it was, until Christmas Day arrived. Nobody was there to see me, so I succumbed to a hearty session of self-pity and a good long cry. I was pathetically studying the contents of the refrigerator to see what there was to eat when I heard the knock on the door. There he stood, having obviously slipped away from somebody's Christmas, wearing a suit, with a plate of turkey and dressing in his hand and a concerned look on his face.

"I can't stay long," he explained, handing me the plate. Then, probably in reaction to my red eyes and tear-stained face, he added, "How about you get out of here for a while? Come on. I'll take you for a ride."

I followed him wordlessly to his car, and he drove way out into the country, to a place where nothing was visible but blinding white Wisconsin expanse and a stubble of bare trees on the horizon. He left the motor running so the heater would work, put his arm around me, and let me cry some more on his overcoat. Then he brought me back.

I think we became friends then, and that promised to last longer than the lover part. And so it did, as it turned out.

Nevertheless, things heated up again when I moved to Minneapolis, far away from the watchful eyes of Patti/Nana. By that time the comedy team was fully involved in touring the college circuit with their act. When they were to play a school within range of Minneapolis, or when they appeared at a comedy club in the Twin Cities, they stayed with me. I had a colorless, utilitarian two-bedroom apartment near Lake Calhoun, but it was cozy enough to make some incredible memories. The singer slept in the guest room, but the comedian slept with me. Through many magical nights he sprinkled his pixie dust and taught me how to fly past the "second star to the right and straight on 'til morning."

Once when he left I found his black turtleneck in my bed, and I was glad. By this time I had already begun to make the connection between him and Peter Pan, and I laughed and thought, "Now I have his shadow," so that, however long it might be, he wouldn't forget to come back again to reclaim it.

For a couple of years, he didn't forget. Sometimes he would even show up in the rest of my life in Minneapolis. Once he came to a show I directed for a little group of actors on the St. Paul campus of the University of Minnesota, where I taught to earn my assistantship. They were not exactly practiced theater students, or they wouldn't have been on the "farm campus," as it was called. U. of M.-St. Paul was home to the agriculture, home economics, and veterinary majors. The student drama club called themselves the Punchinello Players and had a modest

The Place Just Right

little theater-in-the-round constructed in an old classroom. We thought it might be fun and campy to do *Dracula*. The play, being very old, was written for a proscenium theater where certain effects can be hidden from the audience, things like bats flying into the room, as a case in point. We tortured over how to do that, finally coming up with a sort of "bat track" that was suspended along with the lights above the actors in their circular space. It worked on a primitive sort of pulley system. During several rehearsals it worked just fine. The bat appeared on cue from one of the aisles, flew around the stage, and disappeared, creating, with the help of the actors' reactions, the desired horrifying effect.

On opening night disaster struck. In the first place, somebody had invited some inner-city high-school classes to the performance. I had forgotten that teenage girls are prone to screaming and stomping when they are thrust into darkness, and our play had a lot of darkness. The dated script, even though we had cut it mercilessly, was nevertheless still too wordy for that audience, and worst of all, when it came time for the bat to enter, it jumped the track, quivered, trembled some in the air, and fell with a thud into the middle of the stage. By the time the play was over, I was mortified—rigid with embarrassment. It was one of the worst things I have ever experienced in theater. Peter Pan got me out of there as soon as possible and took me to some restaurant for a drink.

We sat in stony silence for at least thirty minutes, and then he started, softly at first, then louder and louder as I began to become aware of what he was doing. He re-created the whole production in sound effects, and it was brilliant. The screams, the stomps, the wolves baying in the distance, touches of the wooden dialogue, and finally, the bat. He spent a long time on the bat—flip-flapping along the track, squealing around the critical turn, jumping the track, quivering and trembling, and finally, the crash, the thud and death throes in the middle of the stage. Re-created perfectly. By the time he was done, I was shrieking with laughter.

Everyone knows how *Peter Pan*, the story, ends. Forgetful Peter comes to Wendy's window less and less frequently, distracted by his never-ending childhood adventures. And Wendy? Well, she has to grow up, like it or not. The day came when I told him I was moving out of the colorless, utilitarian apartment and in with Jon, the man who would in due time become my husband. For a long minute he seemed surprised— uttered a profanity. Then he wished me luck.

Over the years we saw each other a few times. I would catch their act now and then at various places; he came to see us once when we were in New York and took pictures of our little boy. He showed up as well at Sardis's in New York, the one and only time I ever got to have an opening night there, for a little musical I was stage-managing, brought to New York from North Carolina. He loved tagging along that night, soaking up the atmosphere. My North Carolina friends kept asking, "Who's that guy?" as he cracked wise about this and that. Once I ate fettuccine Alfredo with him and his new wife in their apartment near Lincoln Center. I was not a great guest, unusually distracted that trip with my own problems and finding it weird as well to see him, apparently, so domesticated. It was out of character. Peter Pan just doesn't get married.

The comedy team never became stars, although they sniffed around the edges of it, making several appearances on late-night TV, and along the way, playing some pretty good clubs. And Peter Pan had a wonderful twenty minutes or so in a very good movie, cast as a bouncer being taunted by another actor in a long, extremely funny monologue. He doesn't say much, but I like to watch it anyway on occasion.

In the movies, as everybody knows, people never, never grow old.

Moving to L.A.

With Jon and our son, David, at our first home in Los Angeles.

When I was growing up in Eaton, well-meaning people would ask me, "Are you going to be a teacher like your mother?" I came to dread the question. It seemed inconsiderate, not to mention incessant. I could barely hide the surliness in my voice when I answered, "No." I wasn't the kind of child who aspired to follow in my mother's footsteps. I wanted to be my own person, not a carbon copy of somebody else.

The irony is, of course, I have spent more of my working life teaching than doing anything else. I absolutely detested every moment teaching in a village high school right out of college. But in the context of the educational theater, it wasn't so bad. It is a lot easier to teach in a college than in a high school. And it is a lot easier to teach something you love. Still, teaching is not doing, as Jon and I both discovered in North Carolina.

Many of our classmates from Minnesota went immediately to New York or Los Angeles after graduation to try their luck as professionals in theater or film. However, Jon and I seemed to be among the academics, cultivated by our professors as Ph.D. scholars, crammed full of dramatic literature, theater history, and criticism. When Jon received an offer from the University of North Carolina, we got married and went off to the land of mockingbirds and magnolias. It took us five years to realize, although it couldn't be called a mistake, it was not to be our final stop.

For four years life in North Carolina was charming. The town was quaint, the foliage lush, and the climate perfection. We became bird-watchers, waking up early on spring weekends to search out the towhee, the brown creeper, or our favorite, the white-throated sparrow. We had a male dog named Margaret and a wise, even profound, chuckwalla lizard named Joan. Eventually, we bought a brand-new house with a creek and woods in view and were blessed with a beautiful baby boy. Our parents came to visit, beaming with joy and relief that we had finally landed somewhere respectable, our futures, for all intents and purposes, secured.

Jon worked with graduate students who were replicas of the ones we knew in Minneapolis—intelligent, talented, and witty, albeit with Southern accents. I found interesting little theater companies in the community and, eventually, a job at a college nearby. But we should have seen the warning signs—although we loved the graduate students, we never felt comfortable with the faculty. There seemed to be something peculiar about each one of them, except for the one or two who still carried with them the freshness of the last place they had been.

This is what we couldn't articulate about the academic theater as we were living it in North Carolina among the magnolia blossoms and wisteria in the mid-'70s. The professional theater lives or dies by attracting the attention of contemporary audiences. It flourishes best in places where ideas are whirling about and bumping against each other, where streets are full of people and issues are alive in restaurants, bars, and clubs. But academic theater, produced in sedate, vine-covered buildings, under spreading shade trees and across soft, green lawns, quickly loses its vitality and meaning except as nostalgia and tradition. And people who make theater, once they have shared what they know and the best things they can create, need to go back to the mainstream for inspiration, or they quickly become irrelevant.

Brash and confident when we arrived in North Carolina, we immediately spotted the irrelevancies of other members of the faculty. Some were simply stuck in time, like the Southern gentleman who wore white suits, was obsessed with Emily Dickinson, and was a standing joke every morning when he made his rounds of the offices asking, "Had your mornin' coffee?" Another, humorless and glowering, was famous for a dictatorial step-by-step style of direction, totally anachronistic in the freewheeling '70s. Several others simply drank too much, barely hiding whatever private regrets and demons possessed them.

It was all too easy to spot the irrelevancies of others. What were more difficult to notice were the inevitable irrelevancies of our own, quickly beginning to sprout in the isolation of the lush, bucolic South. The honeymoon period ended; the graduate students we loved earned their degrees and left. Newer faculty came to share or hog the spotlight, and the enduring things that never change on a campus—the scholarship, the lectures and seminars, the pressure for publication and for measuring up to tenure—seemed too dull and plodding to define a future, even in such a safe green setting.

The magnolia blossoms began to brown, the wisteria vines to tangle, and the song of the mockingbird to grate and irritate. Our lives no longer felt charmed. So we sold the brand-new house with a view of a creek and woods, held a yard sale, and, with our beautiful baby boy whining and complaining most of the way, packed up a U-Haul with our remaining belongings and headed for Los Angeles, our futures clouded by smog.

Not For Profit

Ruth Ann, Sharon, and Rosalie were only being generous. They had purchased a subscription to a theater in Dayton as a party of four, and number 4 was unable to go to the next event, a musical. Would I like to take her place? My first impulse was to say no.

The truth is I am uncomfortable in the audience of a theater, having no role other than to enjoy the show, which, unless it is uniquely and surprisingly wonderful, I wouldn't. Too many years on the other side of the curtain have robbed me of my innocence. However, since I couldn't say as much without sounding like a snob, and since I didn't want to seem ungrateful to such nice ladies, I said yes instead, hoping the experience wouldn't be too painful.

Strange as it may sound after years in the educational theater, my education about theater didn't really begin until Jon and I finally left college campuses for Los Angeles. We weren't uneducated about the process of breaking in. What we hadn't learned in classes we had learned from friends who had arrived there first. We knew perfectly well we had left the ethereal world of truth and beauty for the business of selling ourselves.

Jon immediately set about doing what aspiring actors do: preparing and distributing résumés, auditioning for showcase theaters, and badgering agents and casting directors any way he could. He loved film and television. Always had. Which is why we were in Los Angeles instead of New York. I, on the other hand, was not suited for film or television, so I focused on the theaters. I knew Los Angeles was full of actors and directors scrambling all over themselves and each other for a chance to be noticed. So I shelved any ambitions I might have had in those areas. Rather, having done almost every job in theater, I called around offering to volunteer in production for the opportunity of getting acquainted with theater in L.A.

It wasn't long before I was sitting by the side of the director of the ninety-nine-seat Odyssey Theatre Ensemble as general "gofer" for a production of *The Threepenny Opera* by Bertolt Brecht. One thing led to another. Through the director of the Odyssey Theatre, I became involved with the Los Angeles Theatre Alliance, a membership organization of fifty small theaters which provided a variety of services for its members. Through the Alliance I got to know every theater producer in Los Angeles and large numbers of actors and directors. Through them I had a front-row seat to the day-by-day operation of dozens of struggling professional theaters in a town dominated by the film and television industries. That was my education. It was a bumpy ride. That's the way it is in the arts. Nothing is ever easy.

The fifty theaters of the Los Angeles Theatre Alliance were the unruly siblings of one large, well-known, heavily subsidized regional theater complex in downtown Los Angeles. A theater complex able to pay its actors a full union (Equity) wage. Like most cultural institutions in America today, it was a not-for-profit organization. The other theaters were even more literally not-for-profit since Equity, in order to prevent the exploitation of its actors/members, refused to allow the actors to perform without full wages at any theater with a hundred seats or more. A show has to have a very long run to make a profit from fewer than a hundred customers a performance.

The theaters I knew in Los Angeles were small and struggling, yet most were lively places devoted to a chaotic variety of artistic visions. Some provided a safe harbor for experiments in playwriting or visionary acting styles; some were principally ethnic or gay. A few were striving to evolve into bona fide theater institutions that kept full repertory companies and paid their actors a living wage. There were improvisational comedy troupes and companies of famous or semifamous or formerly famous movie actors keeping in acting shape by doing theater. There were theaters that offered classes and workshops to keep going. Some were blatant showcases for aspiring movie actors to display their talents to casting directors and agents. I loved them all.

Little theaters are an important breeding ground for new ideas and talent. The film industry and television depend on them for fresh faces. I remember all too well when Robin Williams was discovered in a small improvisational comedy group. At the Los Angeles Theatre Alliance, we always felt that the moguls of the film industry ought to be more generous to the theaters since they provide so much talent for the movies. Somehow, they never quite saw it that way, so the great divide between rich and poor remains.

Like other not-for-profit organizations, the fortunes of the Los Angeles Theatre Alliance went up and down year by year. In good times we all got paid—in bad times I would go to work for a temp agency until things got better. Finally, the Alliance folded, and I became the manager for one of the classier of our ninety-nine-seat theaters until I finally left theater for good.

I went to the musical in Dayton with my friends with a sense of detachment and curiosity. Later, I even attended a nearby dinner theater with the Lakengren Women's Club. But I am still not a very good audience member. My friends and I have quite different reactions to the experience. Here, in the boonies, most shows are designed to be audience pleasers. They are tested properties, comedies and musicals with easily recognizable titles. The noise level is high, singers heavily miked for older audiences, and the physical stage business broad and contrived for laughs. My friends made it clear that foul language or overt sexuality easily offended them. I presume they are typical local subscribers, so the local producers need to be conservative. What was a novelty for my friends was, however, generally a yawn for me. Sitting through a shortened, loud, and frenetic production of *Show Boat* in a dinner theater filled with senior citizens, I learned, is not my favorite way to spend an afternoon. Even the music couldn't redeem it.

There was, however, something that made me smile. During the intermission I opened the program to the cast bios. I was astonished at how young and inexperienced the cast members were. The leads seemed to have in their credits one or two productions outside of the area, indicating some experience in regional theaters, but the bulk of the cast was straight out of college. When the production resumed, I watched them more closely. They had obviously been put through their paces many times during the run of the show, but I could tell they were loving every intense, earnest, energetic moment they were privileged to be on that stage. It would be a fair credit on their résumés, especially at this stage of their careers. I am rooting for every one of them. I hope they make it big.

San Fernando

The dingy hall of the second floor of San Fernando High School still echoed with the sound of student voices returning to class from lunch, even though the crowd had begun to thin—disappearing reluctantly into the open classroom doors. As I stood at the entrance to room 239, watching for stragglers, I was surprised to hear among the usual shouts and laughter the faint but unmistakable crow of a rooster. "What next?" I thought.

I looked in the direction of the now more obvious commotion. From around the corner at the top of the stairs, two boys appeared vainly trying to cover up the fact that they were carrying four large boxes covered with cloth. These were the source of not only the crowing, but a variety of clucking and other chicken-like noises as well. They hustled them past me into my room and quickly rushed them to the back table, where they stuck their heads under the covers and made soothing and comforting sounds to the fowl inside.

I loved teaching public speaking. Every day was a new adventure.

There aren't many classes taught in inner-city high schools in which students are encouraged to express themselves or share their interests with the teacher and fellow classmates. Unfortunately, as I quickly learned, much of what inner-city teenagers really like—their music, their art, their taste in clothes and jewelry, their heroes and role models—they mostly don't talk about in front of teachers and administrators, especially white ones. They can smell judgment and disapproval a mile away. Unless, of course, they deliberately want to try to shock somebody. Then they flaunt it.

Public speaking, however, particularly the requisite "show and tell" activity, is worthless if heavily censored. The kids learned best when they put their enthusiasms and tastes in front of each other and got a real reaction from their peers. Besides, I discovered long ago in such classes, I always had something to learn from the students. So except for things that were obviously illegal—pornography; bongs, pipes, and other drug paraphernalia; and anything that might possibly be construed as a weapon—most subjects were fair game.

When San Fernando High School went year-round, and I was moved upstairs to room 239, some subjects became a little harder to accommodate. But with the ingenuity of the kids, we managed. In previous years, when I taught in 116, the first-floor room with the little stage, all sorts of fascinating and questionable things had simply been sent through the window from the lawn that bordered the street outside—things the kids preferred not to try to sneak past the dean's office near the first-floor entrance. Among these were: trays of tamales and vats of posole; boom boxes and tape players for music demonstrations; exercise mats and sports equipment; little sisters and brothers destined for new hairdos or makeup demonstrations; spray cans and butcher paper designed to show off a variety of tags; kittens, goldfish, and, once, a pit bull puppy.

The fighting roosters, however, were something I had never seen before. I learned a lot that day. Of course, we couldn't permit an actual fight, but we all got to see how it works. The boys had prepared a thorough demonstration including the fancy little hoods that are placed over the eyes, the horrifying spurs for the feet, the rules of the game, the wagers. As the class and I watched with fascination two macho boys dressing their birds for battle, I was reminded of nothing so much as little girls dressing their Barbie dolls to go out in their tiny shoes and hats. I think the class learned a great deal that day as well. We had a lively discussion on the ethics of the issue when they were done. The kids take this sort of thing much better from each other than they do from a teacher.

My students loved public speaking; that is, once they got over their stage fright. When they came back to visit after graduation, it was always the first thing they mentioned.

When I began teaching in 1961 in Preble County, Ohio, I had no idea what I was doing. Teaching high school is one of the most complex activities in the world. It is much, much easier to teach in a college—a piece of cake, as a matter of fact. All that is required is that you know something and can tell it to a room full of people. I have seen dozens of new teachers walk into classrooms in a high school thinking it will be the same there. I have seen almost as many walk out never to return—wondering what went wrong. In their anger and humiliation, they blame everyone from the students to the parents to television and the media to the administration to the system. An irony about my teaching career is that at Lewisburg High School, eight miles from Eaton, three of my most difficult students, from a family of recent immigrants from Kentucky and the only students from that time whose faces I remember, came from people who loved cockfighting. I was horrified. I never let them talk about it. Much more important in those days were the differences between nouns and verbs, pronouns and adverbs. I think I knew better by the time I left teaching for good.

Home Again

A few days back I stopped into Gary's Pharmacy, part of a low complex of offices on Eaton Lewisburg Road as it begins to turn into country heading northeast out of town. Eaton Lewisburg is my favorite country road. I like that it is narrow with both trees and farmhouses very close. Instead of having to look across a cornfield into the lives of the farmers, on Eaton Lewisburg Road I seem to be cutting through their front yards. If I drive slowly enough to be noticed, cows will come to the fence and stare, and a dog might bark.

Gary's Pharmacy is well aware it is on the edge of country. The entire outer third of the store is filled with country kitsch: red or blue and white mottled plates and crocks and coffee cups; cozies and caddies made like farm roosters and cows; three-foot-high stuffed figures—animal and human—in calico and bonnets; and seven varieties of fudge laid out on the checkout counter under waxed paper. The stationery and notepad pages are so filled with renderings of kittens, birdhouses, watering cans, and trailing morning glory vines it is impossible to find a clean space to write the messages for which they were intended.

The pharmacist at the back of the store has given me a bag of medication and a receipt to take to the cashier up front by the fudge, only he has stapled the receipt to the bag in such a way as to render it unreadable. The cashier has to rip it open again and restaple. Instead of showing any kind of irritation, she rolls her eyes, smiles gently, and confides that this pharmacist is retired except for two mornings a week. Although they have explained and explained how he should staple the receipt, he just forgets.

My mind flashed back to my pharmacist grandfather who at eighty-six, although no longer filling prescriptions, was still waiting on people in his

The Place Just Right

drugstore. He would bring writing tablets instead of cold tablets to customers because he didn't hear so well anymore. That drugstore too was filled with kitsch, the tourist variety: six-inch replicas of pine privies and racks of postcards, earrings and lockets bearing the words *Vermilion, Ohio*. Although it didn't often please the tourists from Cleveland, efficiency took a backseat to compassion in my grandfather's drugstore. It still does at Gary's Pharmacy.

On that same trip I stopped into a hardware store to purchase a snow shovel. My wallet is poorly designed, and as I struggled to get the change out of an awkward pocket, I turned to apologize to the man behind me for taking too much time. "You're just fine, ma'am," he said with a smile. Like Gary's semiretired pharmacist and my grandfather, I am lucky to be growing old here instead of in Los Angeles or New York.

Since I have been back in Ohio, many things have charmed me. I saw six covered bridges in one day, each one spanning a small creek or run that gurgled softly under the rough planks. They were hard to find because my map was small and crude. Each one was far from a state road, so removed sometimes it felt like I was intruding on the privacy of a farm family. Signs were missed, roads passed and retraced. It was hot, and at one point the skies opened in a sudden but short overflow of heavy rain, leaving the summer air so damp, steam was rising from the roads and fields. Reaching each bridge was like finding a jewel in the mist.

There is a family of cardinals in our small woods along the cove who have finally started coming to the feeder. The first was a young female that jerked and hopped and was so unkempt in feather and crest that her name evolved from Scuzz to Scuzzie to Scuzette to Scuzerella. She is neater now and comes with Sis and Mom every morning around ten o'clock. The kids go into their act. They open their mouths and twitch their feathers until Mom sticks something in their beak. She's a sucker. They are much too old for that. After a while, Dad comes by and scatters all the nonentities at the feeder with his beauty and dignity.

More than once in my life, after struggling through what I considered a very personal and difficult life decision, I have come upon an article or commentary that confirmed my worst, most humbling suspicions. What I had decided to do, and thought so considered and unique, was only one example of a national trend.

This was true when I joined the exodus of millions of young people from small towns to cities in the sixties, again when I drifted out of the Midwest into the Sun Belt, as far as California. When the population shifted, so did I. Now I find it has happened again. In the Information Age there is a new exodus, out of cities and back to small-town life, often by retirees, but by others as well. So here I am—a refugee from Los Angeles in rural America, like so many others. I still like to think my reasons were unique, but I suspect they were not. The best that can be said for them is that they were maybe a year or two ahead of the pack, but well behind the pioneers.

There exists, I believe, in each generation a collective psyche created by shared experiences and events that in turn create similar yearnings, needs, repulsions, and attractions among its members. We are all pushed and pulled along in the wake of our common history. Therefore, it is not puzzling that, spontaneously, with no apparent connection between them, isolated artists of a given time will begin to create literature or art forms that are both new yet similar in content and form to each other. The human heart swings like a pendulum from one need to another as the old satisfactions become cloying, insufficient, or painful. The small town—once confining, a prison of the mind, a bigoted, provincial backwater with scant nourishment for body or soul—at a later stage of life becomes a refuge from pseudosophistication, hypocrisy, bureaucracy, tension, and world-weariness.

So I am thrown up onto the shores of Lake Lakengren, deposited by my generation's own peculiar historical tides, and what do I find? Amazingly enough—I find joy. Since the last few years have not provided much of this particular sensation, I have trouble recognizing it, but I am confident joy is what it is.

Sometimes it comes on me quietly; something that barely seemed out of whack, but must have been, settles in. Like the quiet relief when a chiropractor performs an adjustment and eases the discomfort. Sometimes it is an amazing surprise—a sight, a delight that jerks a nerve or two alive and starts current flowing to turn on a laugh, or at least, a sudden smile or exclamation. Often it is affirmation. A contented sigh of pleasure or relaxation of the muscles of neck and shoulder. It is a hum of harmony, a whiff of beauty, a taste of a sweet idea brewing. It is a gift in the mail, and perhaps it is marked *fragile* and will not last. But for now, I accept it gladly.

Lakengren

State Route 732 follows a twisted course southwest from Eaton. The entrance to Lakengren, my community, is partially hidden beyond a curve in the road and comes as a surprise when, like a thunderstorm in May, it suddenly pops up out of nowhere. It is an incongruous appearance. State Route 732 is typically rural, passing through acres of soybean and cornfields and by delightful, decaying barns and sturdy white farmhouses.

I have developed a familiar affection for some of the farmhouses; although, unlike my uncle Buzz, I don't know who lives there or who lived there fifty years ago or what became of them when they left. I watch as I pass for the old woman at the mailbox, the felled tree that looks like a dead horse and the hex sign over the wide, grassy entrance to an apparently unused magnificent barn. The jagged road is usually free from traffic, but one late afternoon I counted seventy-five cars coming as I was going after the workday. It is peculiar to see that train of automobiles in the middle of the country.

The entrance to Lakengren is long and graced by the presence of two enormous green and yellow wooden sea serpents that hover on either side of the gate area. Streets follow a faux Scandinavian theme—names such as Thor, Viking, and Fiord Drive. The gate is manned by a succession of cheerful people who, as my brother-in-law sarcastically put it, "keep the riffraff out." Even in the heartland, maybe especially in the heartland, fear of the unknown persists, and many retirees live here.

It is one of the moral dilemmas of our overpopulated times. How can I choose to live in a place that selects who comes in the gate and who does not? Furthermore, isn't there something slightly crass about inhabiting what is essentially a suburban development on an artificial lake that intrudes on and threatens to change forever the traditional rural and small-town atmosphere? To be correct, I should have restored some old farmhouse, or at least one of the fallen-on-hard-luck traditional houses in town—assuming, of course, I had the means or the energy to do it.

That, however, is a big-city, liberal argument that would bring a condescending smile around here. Frankly, though it crosses my mind, it doesn't cause me to lose much sleep. After all, Lakengren is not a particularly rapacious place, having been here already twenty-five years, showing no signs of growing clones or spawning shopping centers, and still possessed of a generous number of undeveloped lots (although only a few now on the waterfront). Lakengren is generally considered a blessing and a boon to all the plumbers, contractors, roofers, painters, and other working-class people who make up the bulk of Eaton's population. It also helps to know that the "riffraff" in question around here are teenagers who like to get drunk and knock down country mailboxes with baseball bats. It is, after all, the prettiest place to be in the region. So we uneasily resolved the issue. Or shoved it under the rug.

Lakengren operates with an elected volunteer board of directors that conducts its business through a variety of committees—also volunteer. When I was approached to join one of those committees, in this case the committee in charge of the dam, my uncle Buzz came out with one of his most memorable lines. "I wouldn't be on any Damn Committee!" he insisted. Since then, in our vocabulary, any committee here, including the board of directors, is automatically—the Damn Committee.

My house is on the waterfront, sort of, perched above a little finger or cove of the lake. It has the advantage of distance from the din of Jet Skis and waterskiers in the summer. In the winter the lake level is lowered deliberately, and fully one-third of my little cove becomes a muddy flat. The docks for the boats reveal their long, heron-esque legs, and the newly denuded dirt-brown border at the sides of the cove becomes dressed again in streaks of ice and snow.

The raccoons and chipmunks disappear, replaced by hordes of juncos and annoying flocks of English sparrows, grackles, and mourning doves—trash birds that must have followed us all the way from Los Angeles. There is no gate to keep

The Place Just Right

that riffraff out. But there are also titmice, blue jays and cardinals, red-bellied and downy woodpeckers and flickers who keep things classy, if somewhat loud and boisterous. And there are the Canada geese. Although I understand that the Damn Committee tries to keep them away (the latest idea: a twenty-foot fake alligator in the lake), they seem to come and go at will. Sometimes an entire congregation of them gather in the sky, and with a great group bellow, head off together. I am sure they have migrated until a day or so later, little packs of them, or perhaps a new flock from the north, reappear over the horizon or paddle about in the two-thirds of our cove that isn't mud flat. Of all the bird sounds from my youth, I remember most the honk of the Canada goose—rude and unashamed, proud and desultory at the same time.

Lakengren has pockets of exceptional beauty, one visible from the patio door of my bedroom. As the cove contorts into a sharp Z on its way to the main lake, the land at its edge flattens out and takes on the guise of a civilized, genteel park with willow trees and blue spruce placed on the canvas at proportionate intervals and colorful boats parked at wooden docks on the water. The homes across the way on Plunder Cove, their best faces toward the water, add to the illusion of upper-class elegance.

Preble County, Ohio, like traditionally agricultural areas all across America, struggles very hard these days to preserve both its rural and small-town cultures, and at the same time, maintain a healthy, developing economy. The twice-weekly *Register-Herald*, in strident editorials and letters to the editor, reflects the divisions and concern of the citizens and officials about the often-incendiary issues of development, rezoning, and conservation. These are not easy situations, and there is no clear moral high road.

Lakengren is symbolic of that ambiguity, a suburban/resort/retirement community of about twenty-five hundred souls behaving like a small town in the middle of the country. Personally, I like that it is motley and poorly defined. It makes living here a lot more interesting.

The Eaton Place

Not long ago, I had lunch with my high-school friend and baton twirler Betty Jane at the Eaton Place, a low, brown wooden building just off Eaton Lewisburg Road across from the cheap apartments at the north edge of town. I was pleased she would come out. I knew she socialized very little of late.

Every small town has such a diner. My friend Charnell calls it the "spit and whittle" spot where the good ole boys hang out. The booths, tables, and counters were all packed when Betty Jane and I arrived. It took a while to get a seat.

The Eaton Place was not here when I was growing up, but Uncle Ben tells me it has been around for a very long time. One of his favorite stories on his social worker wife, my mother's older sister, Eleanor, is that when she would go there for lunch, the room, and most particularly the cops invariably sitting at one of the center tables, would go absolutely silent. Aunt Eleanor, at least according to Ben, was something of an Avenging Angel in Eaton marching into the most disreputable of places, removing children if necessary, enforcing order and justice with impunity. Even the police behaved themselves in her presence, not entirely sure how she was entitled to do what she did or certain what she might do next.

That is, of course, Ben's version of it. He might have exaggerated a bit. He also had her rum-running during the war, obtaining hard-to-get spirits here and there as she made her rounds in and out of shady neighborhoods. Given Eleanor's quiet demeanor and moral idealism, that is very hard to believe. Still, it is touching to hear him talk about her with such pride and admiration, especially since my memories of them as I was growing up were that he, Ben, was clearly the dominant figure in their household—barking orders, holding forth on this or that topic while she faded into the wallpaper.

The Place Just Right

I noticed the other day on the generally bare walls of Ben's room at the assisted living facility, that he, or perhaps one of his children, had hung a large picture of Eleanor when she had been May Queen at Earlham College in the '30s. She was the beauty of the family, and the picture is stunning. He doesn't complain, but I know he misses her very much. She died of cancer several years ago.

These thoughts chased around in my mind as I sat across the booth from my old buddy Betty Jane and glanced around for the table where, perhaps, the police went silent at the entrance of my aunt Eleanor all those years ago. I thought about the nearly sixty-year marriage of my other maternal aunt and uncle, Ruth and Buzz, a couple whose relationship is still so fresh and joyous that a guest who recently stayed at their house reported she heard them giggling in bed in the morning. I recalled the surprise and embarrassment I felt when, as a teenager, I happened into the kitchen in Vermilion and caught my grandparents kissing! I was jolted back into the present when I heard Betty Jane say to me, referring to her broken marriage, "We had so much, and he just threw it all away."

In this small Midwestern town, a town in which the *Register-Herald* frequently publishes pictures of sturdy couples, shoulder to shoulder, celebrating their golden wedding anniversaries, is it any wonder that my old friend is confused, amazed, and humiliated? Women, especially women of our age, are never really prepared to be facing life alone, living with our children or in some strange apartment or house without the presence of the only person who truly shares decades of common memories. Or if the predicament of life alone is inevitable, it should at least be more naturally because of death, not the crushing, deliberate choice of a so-called husband. Surely, in such a circumstance, even tragedy is easier to face than abandonment. I want to rail at the universe for my friend. I want to rail at the universe for all women, of all ages (and I think even today they are legion) who stand in the middle of the crystal shards of broken trust from some man, looking for a way to live alone with a modicum of enthusiasm and self-esteem—and without daily tears.

There is a section in Helen Hooven Santmyer's *...And Ladies of the Club* in which one of the main characters discovers that her beloved and much admired husband, a doctor, has been carousing habitually at the local saloon and whorehouse. Everyone seemed to know about it but her. In this case an excuse is made: He has been traumatized by the horrors he has seen in the Civil War, and although he loves his wife, is nevertheless compelled to exorcise his demons through sex and whiskey. But the pages, almost too painful to read, are not about him. They are about her, the wife lying in her marriage bed throughout a long, sleepless night consumed with the agony of betrayal, frantically considering her options, silently playing out one scenario after another on the ways she could or should respond to what she knows. In the end she does nothing. She swallows the molten rock of her pain and anger and goes on about her life as though she had never learned what she learned. But she is not the same person, and it is not the same marriage. As Stephen Sondheim wrote in *A Little Night Music*, "every day a little death." As Midwestern children of the '40s and '50s, neither Betty Jane nor I knew many examples of women who faced their anger with men head-on, or even dared to admit it. Certainly, my own mother was traumatized by my father's misbehavior; apparently, according to family legend, rendered nearly immobile from pain, confusion, and disappointment. It was my grandmother Frances who urged her to leave him. So she crept back to 824 North Maple Street, me in tow, to a house now inhabited by her own recently widowed mother, to the curiosity of a small town and the pity of her friends, and became a schoolteacher instead of the poet I believe she truly wanted to be. She regained her pride, her self-respect, even a zest for life and adventure—but I think her muse forsook her. She avoided music and any other indulgence of sentiment for the rest of her life, as though she were protecting a sore spot deep inside. The walking wounded. There are probably far more of them among the sisterhood than anyone wants to admit, especially among women of my generation. I hope the ones who follow are doing better, but I am not yet convinced they are.

Still, some do rise to the occasion, and did even then. Aunt Maxine, wife of my father's pompous and supercritical congressman brother, Dave, is a shining example. When criticized soundly about the preparation of a whitefish that she had taken great pains to cook for a special occasion, Maxine said nothing. Then, after a few days, when the fish was good and ripe, she packaged it up and mailed it to him at the House Office Building in Washington, D.C. I love that kind of spunk, just as I love the ladies who upon hearing that their man is about to leave them for another woman, run out and charge every penny on his Visa, even if tears are running down their cheeks in the dressing room of the department store. There isn't enough of that spirit in the world. Most of us fold like wet rags. Shame on us.

Betty Jane and I had our meal and our chat. I had a breakfast omelet; she opted for a sandwich from the lunch menu. We laughed and reminisced about high school: the peculiar, crinkly, smelly hair of our classmate Sheila, now dead, bless her heart; the big boobs of some girl we tried to avoid bumping into in the group shower after gym class; the incipient juvenile delinquency of the Mendenhall kid, who, with the Neileigh boy, would leap out of the alley and scare the bejesus out of Betty Jane as she walked home at night past the old Kroger store on Main Street; how Jane Coffman fell off her bicycle twice in five minutes on the very day she got her first period. We agreed to get together more often. It is important, very important, for a woman to have female support. We were that kind of friends for each other once, many, many years ago. Surely we can be again. Forty years may see the ruin of a marriage or two, but it's nothing between girlfriends.

Part III

'TIS THE GIFT TO BE LOVING

'TIS THE BEST GIFT OF ALL
LIKE THE WARM SPRING RAIN
BRINGING BEAUTY WHEN IT FALLS
AND AS WE USE THIS GIFT
WE MIGHT COME TO BELIEVE
IT IS BETTER TO GIVE
THAN IT IS TO RECEIVE

Nice to Remember

> *Deep in December it's nice to remember*
> *The fire of September that made you mellow.*
> THE FANTASTICKS, 1960

Warren Staebler's letter contained an unusual request. Receiving it, in fact, became one of those little things in life that happen at just the right time to make a difference.

Warren, who died not long ago, was an English professor at Earlham College. He and his wife, Patricia, had dragged me, along with a wide-eyed group of college students, through a summer and a semester in Italy in 1960. He had been the epitome of the rumpled, tweedy academic, leading us to all the great art and reciting Chaucer in ancient Roman amphitheaters. She was statuesque and gracious in spite of the tension of having two restless children in tow. Now, he explained in his letter, Patricia was very ill with congestive heart failure. She didn't have much longer to live, he wrote. He felt helpless to do much for her.

He painted a picture of them together in their home, baseball game on television, he making an apple pie as she sat in her recliner chair, able to share with him only the most passive of activities. He thought, perhaps, he could give her some memories to fill her final days, so he was writing to all of the students who had been on that trip, asking that they please write a letter to her sharing their own recollections of that time. I was delighted to comply and did my very best to be vivid and cheerful. Before too long, she answered with gratitude and a few recollections of her own, among them that I had gone through Italy with a knitting basket making continual sweaters. I had forgotten that.

What I didn't tell Patricia, or Warren either, was that here in Ohio, my own life, and Jon's, was slowing down as well, prematurely, like one of those merry-go-rounds in a playground when the adult supposed to be spinning gets distracted. Like stranded children astride the wheel, it was all we could do not to whine for someone to set it in motion again—if only for one or two more spins. The parallel was clear. Patricia sat in her recliner chair, Jon in the wheelchair by the window. Warren made apple pie while the Cincinnati Reds played their game; I worked on meals I hoped would be delicious while the Lakers made their championship runs. But Warren wasn't crying and whining, at least not as far as I could tell. He was collecting memories, and it was definitely mellow.

Warren and Patricia, unknowingly, returned two gifts for my little letter of recollections; one for Jon and me, and one for just me. For us, Warren's example was an assurance that even in the enforced quietude of infirmity, life can be sweet. And so as time went by, Jon and I learned the joy of reliving something old when we could not live something new. He turned out to be a master of the art. We read the old books, listened to old music, looked at pictures and videos, recalled this person or that story, laughed and smiled. It was definitely mellow.

Now I sit at my window watching the west wind grab and tear at the fading yellows and browns of late October, and I revisit my own gift from the Staeblers. Against the gray sky of a dreary day, my memory superimposes the bright hues, light-spattered shadows, and lively cacophony of that long-ago adventure they led me to in Italy. It is indeed nice to remember.

Jon

"Dammit." I spit the word into the sink, slamming the cabinet door.

"What's wrong?" The question came from his usual spot between the table and the northeast window. The morning sun was streaming in, and his voice betrayed just the slightest hint of a grin. I picked it up.

"Okay. Where are they?"

"Where are what?" His voice now absolutely dripped with innocence. His face was contorted trying to hold back the grin.

"My scissors." My teeth were beginning to unclench. I knew what was coming next.

With only a millisecond of a pause, he proudly stated, "Rolling pin." The grin was huge.

I knew exactly what he meant. After all, we had only been through this ten times this month. With a sigh, squelching a smile of my own, I opened the drawer that held the rolling pin and easily spotted the scissors where he had hidden them, lopsidedly placed across the utensil tray in plain sight if only I hadn't fallen for this—yet again.

Jon didn't have enough to do.

I, on the other hand, had way too much to do, which is why I left things out on the counter when I was working and forgot to put them away. Thus setting myself up as the butt of Jon's pranks. Nobody likes to be the butt of a joke, but in this case, I not only forgave him—I was grateful as hell he hadn't lost his capacity for mischief. Things could have been a whole lot worse. Jon coped daily with multiple sclerosis. After I retired from teaching, I got to cope all day with him.

Mischief was a huge part of Jon's personality. When we were first married, I was a slugabed, and in spite of the fact that Jon and I were in theater and up late most nights in rehearsal, he was always awake at the crack of dawn. Sometimes on bright weekend mornings, he would shake me, saying, "Get up—we need to get going—it's already late." Wearily rolling over, I would look at the clock and see it was after ten. I would leap up, get dressed in a rush, and off we would go for breakfast or a bird walk in the forest near campus. Sometime later, at the restaurant or after we had returned home, I would see another clock, and it would be about nine. He had set the clock by the bed ahead by hours, and I had been fooled—again.

Even before we were married, when Jon was in his early twenties, the problems with multiple sclerosis began. In those days, however, it was much harder to get a diagnosis, so it literally took years to discover what really was wrong. There was a sick joke around at the time:

A man is praying to God when suddenly a lightning bolt comes out of the sky and his right hand shrivels up. The man prays even harder. Another lightning bolt comes from the sky and shrivels his left hand as well. This proceeds through all his body parts until the man calls out in desperation, "Oh, God. Why me?" And the answer comes booming out of the heavens, "You piss me off!!!!"

Few religions envision a God who punishes people so capriciously. That's why the joke is funny. But the perversity of the MS and the way it struck, little by little where it hurt the most, made it seem as though surely some angry deity, perhaps Zeus, was up there playing pranks on Jon—in much the same way Jon loved to play them on me. Only these were much meaner.

For instance, Jon had studied classical piano from the time he was a very small boy in New York City. He played very well. When I met him in graduate school, he had already established, along with his best friend, a music major, a tradition of performing two-piano recitals for the theater students. They were eagerly anticipated because both of them performed with a flourish and great joy. It was during the rehearsal period for one of these recitals that several of his fingers went numb. Nearly frantic with frustration and fear, he forced his fingers over the notes again and again as though sheer repetition would bring back normal sensations. By some miracle, the numbness did indeed subside in time for the recital, but it was never satisfactorily explained.

A few years later, when Jon was teaching at the University of North Carolina, the part of the job he relished most was lecturing for the large introductory theater classes. He prepared in the same way he prepared for a performance, with the result that the lectures were colorful and popular with students. So it was especially cruel that the next unexplained neurological incident involved his speech.

His words abruptly began to garble and slur while he was talking. We clocked it with a stopwatch and found that the slurring would almost always occur for thirty seconds every two minutes, coming and going on a pattern of its own—totally beyond Jon's control. While the flummoxed doctors tried to puzzle it out, we desperately rehearsed each lecture, incorporating the pauses required by the involuntary garbling into the text, so the students would be unaware that anything was wrong. Whatever trick was being played on us, by whomever, had our attention. Miraculously again, within three months the slurring subsided into nothing but a memory and never came back.

Relieved that nothing else was happening, in 1977 we left the security of college life for the uncertainty of life in Los Angeles, thumbing our noses at whatever conclusions might have been drawn from either "the fingers thing" or "the speech thing." Nobody should sit around waiting for bad things to happen, and although the words "multiple sclerosis" had indeed been uttered as a possibility, for all we really knew, it could just as well be nothing at all. We were not to be so lucky.

Over the next few years, Jon helped to keep our heads above water financially by proofreading film scripts for a script-typing service. Naturally, since proofreading demands close visual attention to detail, the next thing to happen was to his eyes. This time Zeus wasn't just fooling around. The condition was optic neuritis, known even then to be a strong indicator of MS.

The optic neuritis never got any better, only progressively worse. Eventually, both eyes were affected not only by optic neuritis, which destroys central vision through damage to the optic nerve, but also by nystagmus, an involuntary tremor of the eye that left Jon looking at the world, as he described it, as if he were looking through a bowl of shaking Jell-O. He could see colors and light through that shaking, shimmering film—little else. So much for proofreading.

So much as well for an acting career. I remember vividly one opening night for the little theater company where Jon was a member. He had been assigned to welcome the audience and make a pitch for some upcoming event. As he left his seat and took a small hop up onto the stage to get the attention of the audience, he stumbled and fell flat on his face. Purpose accomplished. Everyone in the entire theater was looking directly at him. That was the first of countless stumbles, lurches, staggers, and weaves across rooms and down sidewalks, topped off by the climactic arrest—the one incident that precipitated more than any other the final recognition that we could not ignore this problem or deal with it any longer in a casual, dismissive way.

It was our son's eighth birthday. Jon had been on an errand, and David and I were waiting for him to come home so we could go out to dinner and celebrate. It was late, and I was starting to worry. When the phone finally rang, I heard a tense and confused Jon on the other end telling me he was at the police station in downtown Los Angeles. His car had been impounded. I left our son in the care of a neighbor and got there as fast as I could. Jon was pale and shaking, obviously scared to death.

His fear was not surprising. After all, this was the Los Angeles police, and Jon had always been unduly terrified by authority figures. Although he was in many ways more courageous than any man I have ever known, this courage did not appear in confrontations with anyone inclined to be dominating or physically aggressive—playground bullies, bosses or department chairpersons, doctors, military personnel of any description—and certainly not the police. Jon's modus operandi in any such confrontation had always been to immediately become obsequious and joke his way out of it. Apparently, the police had not been amused.

I pieced together the story. Jon had been stopped by the officers for weaving on the road. The police had decided he was either drunk or on drugs and became sure of it when they asked him to walk a straight line on the sidewalk. That was impossible, although the breath test showed no signs of alcohol. Clearly, something wasn't right, so they decided to take him down to the station. They had been questioning, testing, and accusing for some time, finally giving up in frustration when it became clear Jon was not on any drugs they could detect. So they released him to me with this less than reassuring statement: "You've got problems, buddy." And so he did. So did we all.

Not long after that, a neuro-ophthalmologist ordered an MRI (at that time still a new procedure), and finally, after over twelve years of suspecting, wondering, and avoiding the issue, we got a definitive diagnosis of multiple sclerosis. Although we struggled mightily not to let it become the dominant factor in our lives, and particularly not in the life of our son, we were not always successful. As the years passed and the disease progressed, it inevitably changed all of our lives irretrievably.

A Eulogy
(Delivered at the First Presbyterian Church in Eaton, Ohio)

I have titled my remarks *Fridays with Ben*.

Last night, after dinner, Cousin Dan invited the guests to share memories of Ben. I went into a small panic. I thought, "There goes my speech for the funeral." Fortunately, no serious damage was done. It brought to mind, however, that there were people there and here today who know some of these stories already, probably better than I do. So, if I am not relating what actually happened, you have to blame Ben, not me. I recorded them faithfully.

It is a wonderfully instructive thing to spend an hour on a quiet afternoon with a man in the final years of his life—the kind of afternoon when the tick of a clock and the rustle of a newspaper are the loudest sounds in the room, and there is time to kill before dinner. I was blessed to do that often with my uncle Ben these past few years. My day to visit was Friday, and if he wasn't too tired or impatient, he would tell me stories. These stories were always preceded with the phrase "Have I told you about the time...?"

I always said, "No, I don't think so." He got so much joy out of telling the story, I just couldn't say I had already heard it—maybe a dozen times or more.

If anyone ever wonders what is important about a human life, and on the occasion of a death most of us do so wonder, then there is much to learn from listening to the stories of elderly men—or women. Time has already filtered out the trivial things, the forgettable, the discardable, and what is left is the essence—the not-so-hidden treasured moments when relived in the telling of a story bring a flash of youthful animation to the old face. I believe the things most important to the life of my uncle Ben are in those stories, in the truth that is undoubtedly there, but also in the embellishments as well. Surely he can be forgiven if he dressed them up a bit over the years. In twenty years who could contradict him anyway? I couldn't.

I was most fascinated by the stories from his youth: high school, college, the war years, coming to Dayton, meeting Eleanor. Young Ben Fieselmann was a new person to me, somebody different from the tall, imposing uncle who made people smile and shake their heads when he hollered "Redhead" to get Aunt Eleanor's attention, and who lined his kids up against the wall at the end of the day to "report" on what happened at school.

Instead of that guy, I got to meet a determined kid so eager to learn that instead of attending the nearest high school, he hitchhiked many miles to another considered the best around. After a few days with his thumb out, he managed to get a regular ride to the school, but it was a new adventure every day getting back home. He stuck it out in Latin class with nothing but girls because somebody told him Latin was important to an educated person. They were quality girls, he told me, of the highest caliber. He remembered most of their names as well as the businesses their fathers ran, and he even could tell me, in fact did, what had become of many of them. He was a stereotype of the Horatio Alger generation: the poor kid, a preacher's kid, on the outside of privilege scrambling to make good and raise his station in life. A kid with persistence and determination and an eye for being at the right place at the right time. I began to admire his spunk. No matter that it could have been embellished for effect. It was still an inspiring story.

It got even better in college. He never tired of talking about his days on the debate team. Debate was once a popular activity on college campuses, and being selected to debate was an honor. Imagine that.

There were several aspirants for a place on the squad who came to him for help in developing the arguments for the topic at hand. According to Ben, he did all the work; they all used his case for their auditions, and when the instructor inquired how they had all come up with the same arguments, they pointed the finger at Fieselmann. (Ben always referred to himself in these stories as Fieselmann. Everyone, it appears, called him simply by his last name.) That is how Fieselmann ended up a pivotal member of the debate team. I especially liked the anecdote that described how, after leaving the scene of a debate, he and his partners were stopped by the police on the highway because one of the debaters (not Fieselmann, certainly) had lifted some towels from the hotel.

It was no exaggeration to say that living through the Depression was a terrible daily struggle, especially for a young person trying to get a start in life. There are so few people left now who had that life-altering experience. Ben was as poor as everybody else, but he manipulated, schemed, and pulled every string he could to get through law school.

Later, one of his law professors accosted him on the steps of the school. "Fieselmann," he said, "come with me," and led him into his office. He then demanded to know how he (Fieselmann), a seemingly mediocre student, could have passed the bar on his first attempt when so many others, apparently brilliant scholars and outstanding individuals, did not. Fieselmann had no certain answer, except to say that he had studied hard and the others were, perhaps, overconfident. I think he applied what he had learned from that experience as a formula his whole life long, clichéd though it be. Work hard and never take anything for granted.

During the early years of the war, Fieselmann found himself a nameless clerk in the Washington bureaucracy. He heard about a newly forming legal group at Wright Patterson Air Force Base. It was clearly not a position, he gave me to understand, that could be applied for in any conventional way. You had to be sought out and asked. Presumably, that is how the military worked in those days—maybe even now. Old friends were contacted, letters written, words exchanged in casual conversation, strings pulled, with the result that, against all odds, Ben Fieselmann came to Dayton, Ohio. Ben took great delight in that episode, told it with relish—outwitting the system, or manipulating it, at any rate.

In spite of the grave historic significance of World War II, life around the base in the '40s as Ben told it sounded, well, fun. There was a clear and noble purpose to the work, there was camaraderie, and there were girls—lots of girls—pretty girls. And everybody wanted to set him up, even with a general's daughter. Ben always had a huge grin when he told that story—the general in civvies opening the door, Fieselmann quaking in his boots. His buddies once brought him six

The Place Just Right

different girls in a row to take out, and then asked him to choose. He picked the redhead who could talk politics. Never mind he was a Republican, and she was a Democrat. The rest was history.

My uncle Ben always gave the appearance of a patriarch: forthright with his opinions, strong, in charge, precise about his wants, and—well—verbal. However, everyone soon came to know who was really in charge. He was a liberated man well before his time—decades before his time. Of course, he admired Eleanor's unusual beauty. "Prettiest girl I ever saw," he said to me, not too long ago, gazing wistfully at the picture of her as college May Queen that always hung in his room. Still, many of his fondest stories were about her, not as a wife and mother, but as a career woman doing her job. To hear him tell it, Eleanor had more power in Eaton than the police, the city council, and the mayor combined. She could accomplish whatever she wanted on behalf of the children she helped, manipulate the system better than anybody. And he was full of pride. Full of pride, too, in his children and grandchildren, cherishing every detail he could learn about their lives and their accomplishments—showing me pictures, quoting from letters, sharing news he learned over the phone.

So what did I learn about the importance of a life from listening to my uncle Ben spin stories all those long, quiet Friday afternoons? I learned that Ben Fieselmann lived his life to become educated, to improve his station and himself, to do a little something for the world and have good cheer while doing it, to cherish his lifelong partner, and to teach his children what he knew. These are the obvious things—the simple things—the important things. And it didn't take me long out in the world to realize what an accomplishment it is to actually do them with dedication, loyalty, and incredible zest a whole life long.

Ben Fieselmann loved his life; he let go of it reluctantly even through illness and loss. He never once complained in my presence about any of those things. To the very end he was reading, learning, talking, and laughing—and he never, as he once said, "descended to bingo."

The last thing he said to me when I left his room at hospice was "See you on Friday." How I wish I could.

Wrestling with Zeus

When I felt impelled to retire to my small Ohio hometown after years in much larger places, I was certain my husband would never agree. He was a New Yorker, for God's sake. He had no history in rural Ohio. What possible appeal could there be for him? I was wrong.

I didn't really understand how few consolations there are for someone with multiple sclerosis who is spending life in a wheelchair: no longer working, no longer able to read, feel comfortable in crowds, or enjoy the attractions of city life. "I want a backyard," he said. "A place where I can feel a breeze, smell living things in different seasons, and hear the birds." That was not affordable on a teacher's retirement in Southern California. It was in Ohio. Jon was happy to come along.

We settled into quiet days and simple activities. We learned new routines, enjoyed different pleasures, and grappled together with his ever-worsening disease.

MS is not a killer—merely a crippler, a thief. Over the years, we have done our best to adjust as MS robbed Jon of one faculty after another—first to canes and walkers, then, finally, the wheelchair. We've adjusted to thick glasses and magnifying devices for seeing, to grab bars and to an accessible toilet; to medications and shots and whatever feeble panacea or harebrained attempt the medical profession has offered to treat an incurable disease.

We have tried to comfort ourselves with the thought that we all lose our faculties someday. This is just a little earlier than most. Tried not to grieve too much or too long as Jon was forced to leave certain precious things behind: driving, the piano (finally), acting, earning a living, reading, leaving the house alone.

The Place Just Right

And we have done our best to adapt as well to the inevitable redefining of roles our predicament required.

I commonly hear people say, when faced with reverses, "When a door is closed, a window opens somewhere." I am not such a Pollyanna as to believe the exchanges in life are always fair, but Jon and I both, reluctantly, have come to understand that valuable lessons come about through loss—lessons that could not be learned any other way. I don't know who the cosmic registrar might be who schedules the classes for anyone's lifetime, but for us, the course of study surrounding MS could have been titled A Practicum on a Descent through Hell and Out the Other Side. It seemed to be a course required for graduation. There was no alternative option or testing out.

In Dante's *Inferno* the very lowest layers of hell, reserved for the most evil souls imaginable, are frozen. Unlike sinners who are blown by fierce winds, who must run forever or writhe in pain, sinners on the bottom are totally immobile, trapped inside rigid, stone-like bodies, condemned to total unresponsiveness and inaction for eternity. One is to suppose that within those icy statues, a consciousness still exists eternally struggling for expression through a still body that cannot speak—cannot so much as raise a finger or blink an eye. This is the ultimate fear from paralysis, or even coma—the claustrophobia of a vibrant spirit trapped inside its body, struggling to get out. And Jon is nothing if not a vibrant spirit—one of the most engaging and energetic I have ever encountered.

The true hell of MS for him, and by extension for me, is not physical pain; MS has very little of that. Nor is it the giving up of accustomed roles, nor even the loneliness of becoming less and less involved with the world, although those are very sad. The true hell for him is the frustration of living in a body that doesn't work.

A nightmare to me is being in another room and hearing him fall. Or catching a glimpse of it happening and being absolutely helpless to prevent it. The falling doesn't happen often, perhaps four or five times a year, but it inevitably occurs in the most awkward places: between the bed and the bars on the wall, for instance, or in the bathroom, wedging him painfully between the toilet and the tub, pants either going on or coming off. On rare occasions it happens at the kitchen sink or in the living room when some unusual thing makes it necessary for him to stand up from the wheelchair. We do everything we can to prevent it, but sometimes it just happens anyway. The legs refuse to hold him up.

The thud or crash comes first, depending on where he hits going down and what might have fallen with him, then a pregnant pause, then the profanity, a stream of it bluer than the language in a prison or an inner-city high school. With this he flails his arms and twists his head and shoulders as if he were in excruciating pain.

Almost immediately we begin yelling at each other: "Let me call 911. I don't see how I'm going to get you out of there."

"No, God damn it. Don't call anybody. Just leave me alone." A lot more blue language.

The next stage is me, on my knees or bending over him, wrestling his legs or arms, trying to get his head out from behind the toilet, or his clothing untwisted or on or off, checking for blood or scrapes and bruises, usually finding some of each. And when the first shock of it all wears off, and we are both a little calmer, we address the question of how he might get off the floor. It is totally beyond my strength to lift him directly. Believe me, I've tried.

In the early years he could usually, eventually, do it himself—dragging his stiff, unbending legs along the floor by his elbows like a soldier creeping through mud with a grenade in his mouth. He would reach a grab bar, or the edge of a heavy piece of furniture and, with a Herculean effort, pull himself up. I would scurry for the chair and put it behind him, and he would drop heavily into it, both of us relieved beyond measure that the crisis was over.

As the disease progressed, he couldn't get up by himself anymore, so it was up to me to figure it out. I could have called 911, I suppose, against his wishes, and humiliated him. But stubbornly, I never have. It became a test of will for both of us—us against fate—determined, somehow, to win another round. Our very own purgatory. Several times it has literally taken hours. We struggle, try things for some minutes, break for refreshment, put on the television, rest and think some, and then go at it again. Once I even brought him a pillow, a blanket, and a cup to pee in and left him on the floor all night. We were both just too exhausted to continue.

After much trial and error, we have gotten better. I learned that if I can get him to the bottom edge of the bed (we have no footboard), and if he can raise his torso enough to flop over it, I can lift his stiff legs and roll them and the rest of him onto the bed. From there it is a cinch. I pull him up to a sitting position and put his legs over the edge of the bed, from where he can reach the grab bars. The same principle applies if I can get him to the large, heavy coffee table in front of the sofa in the living room. There are no grab bars there, but the handles of the wheelchair serve the purpose. Once he is on his feet, he can be flipped around clumsily into the chair from the coffee table. The effort then becomes one of getting him from where he has fallen to one of those two places.

Over time, although he still flails and curses as always, I have begun to panic less and strategize more effectively. I can't lift him, so sometimes I simply roll him, over and over until we get there. If he has fallen in a narrow place, then I drag him, sometimes directly, grabbing his feet and digging in my heels: sometimes, more cleverly, by rolling him on a blanket and dragging that. And finally, the day came when it seemed no longer a crisis but almost—well—normal. We manage. We cope. Together.

Comedy

In graduate school in Minnesota, where Jon and I met, the point was often made (in seminars on Greek tragedy or theory classes in dramatic literature) that tragedy is just a tick away from comedy. In fact, nothing is quite as hilarious as a tragedy badly performed, high seriousness gone awry. In the golden age of Greece, a trilogy of Greek tragedies would be accompanied by a satyr play full of the crudest comedy imaginable. The fall from a high place that constitutes tragedy is barely an inch away from the pratfall.

Surely, that is the reason that in the midst of the panic and physical strain accompanying Jon's falls, I never break into tears. Instead, much to my amazement and embarrassment, I find myself rounding a corner into the next room, just out of Jon's sight, to lean against a wall and shake with suppressed laughter. Laughter at how this would look to an unseen observer, at the stupidity of the predicament, at the ridiculousness of both of us flailing around feebly and uselessly at our situation—at our fate. It is acceptance, I think, for me to be able to laugh. An acknowledgment that neither one of us is important enough in the larger scheme of things to rate the label of tragic hero. This is comedy, indeed.

Although Jon never laughs at his falls (it just makes him too damn mad), as a "funny-as-hell guy from day one," according to his best friend from high school, he certainly finds humor in almost everything else. We howl at the spectacle of our dentist, doing his best to help Jon in and out of the chair, invariably grabbing him by the soft flesh under his arm, causing an excruciating pinch. Jon wanting desperately to cry out but politely sucking up the pain in order not to make him feel bad. Once we were both overcome with giggles at the spectacle of our egotistical neurologist, having rudely taken a call during one of our appointments, holding forth in the foreign language of medical terms and getting stuck on the word *infarct* over and over like a smart-ass kid repeating an obscenity. I had to get up and leave the room, I was laughing so hard; Jon, on the other hand, was stuck there in the chair to explain why we were giggling.

To tell the truth, the literature of MS is full of laughs: people gleefully relating how they became trapped for hours behind the toilet or in the bathtub, fell through plate-glass windows or on a street where they had to be helped up and taken to restrooms by strangers. When Jon was first diagnosed, and I read some of that stuff, I thought they were crazy. They weren't. They had just come out the other side of hell, and we hadn't.

I recently attended a seminar at which a young, successful writer shared an experience that stays with me. She was asked to write a short blurb for another person's book, a very intense accounting of some horrific subject, satanic child abuse, I think. "I wrote it straight," she said. "But all I could think about was how funny I could have made that book." Everyone in the room hooted.

On the other side of tragedy, perhaps on the other side of hell itself, is laughter, humility, and the realization that none of us is so smart or talented, pious or moral as to be spared the fate we are apparently intended to live. I have learned to love this quote from Shakespeare's *King Lear*:

"As flies to wanton boys are we to th' Gods.
They kill us for their sport."

I love it because the probability is high that this is truth. Having faced that down, like the Greek tragic hero, brought low by his own false pride and by the deeply mysterious forces of his own fate, I find a cathartic release and a sense that whatever constitutes cosmic wisdom, I am a little closer to it.

Nycticorax Nycticorax

*M*aybe I can tell this now. Finally now. After treading the salty water of summer, blindly trudging through a drab autumn; after an excruciating Christmas and days of bitter cold; now that it is once again a soft, moist May, and the tall trees behind my house can sway and sing with each approaching spring rainstorm, maybe I can finally talk about it. Not without tears, of course. The tears are a given like the rain. But maybe now the tears won't choke the words quite so much, and I can say it aloud.

It was mid-May when the bird came flying in from the west—low and on a straight course, as if it knew precisely where it was heading. I was stepping out of the car when its huge wings passed me on the left. Startled, I turned to see it land gently in the towering oak tree not far from the back deck. Not down the bank, close to the water, but in a high branch near enough to the bedroom to drop its leaves on the roof in autumn.

I took some packages inside. Then I walked down the long driveway for the mail. Coming back, I noticed its hulking shape in the tree, visible just over the small peak of the roof. "It seems to be settling in," I thought. "That's strange."

When I got inside, I called out, "Jon, there's a different bird in a tree out back!" Although Jon could no longer see well enough to identify its features, he was excited nevertheless. We had done quite a bit of bird-watching in our lives, and it was always thrilling to find something new. He wheeled out on the deck with me as I took a closer look. The bird didn't seem to notice me flipping through the pages of the bird book. Finally, I narrowed it down. Black-crowned night heron (*Nycticorax nycticorax*). "A stocky, nocturnal heron that roosts during the day in trees or marshes, foraging at night in shallow ponds and wetlands... large-headed and short-necked."

The book didn't mention that the black-crowned night heron also possessed stark, staring red eyes made even more obvious by being situated at the ends of gray lines from the lowered black crown of its head to the long beak. However, the picture clearly showed the red eyes, as did my view from the deck. The size of the bird was right, over two feet tall with a wingspan of about forty-four inches. The fact that it was nocturnal explained why it appeared to be settling in for a long daytime nap. That had to be right. There was nothing else quite like it. *Nycticorax nycticorax* it was. We thought the name was rather devilish.

It stayed the entire day. I looked every few hours to be sure. About dusk it left.

It was not long after, shortly before our thirtieth wedding anniversary at the end of May, Jon's first signs of illness appeared. Since a person with multiple sclerosis is always susceptible to weakness, fatigue, bad days, it isn't easy to tell if something new is going on. Jon had never known, not in all the long years he had had MS, whether this condition or that one was related to the disease or something else entirely. As it turned out, he didn't feel pain the same way other people did either. So we coped as usual. He did a little less, slept a little more. I gave him my arm more often, left the house less frequently. He hated being fussed over.

Getting in and out of the car was harder when he wasn't feeling well, but we braved going out to dinner for our anniversary. The restaurant made us comfortable in a patio area outside. We talked. Although we were together now every day, all day, we were never inclined to talk seriously until seated across from each other over a glass of wine and a fine meal. Then the words came pouring out: memories, plans, our son. The occasion seemed normal; except, he couldn't eat. We brought the linguine with clams home for another time.

Had it not been for the eating and the nausea, I don't think we would have gone to the doctor when we did. Multiple sclerosis can make a person sick in a variety of ways, but it doesn't usually make someone sick to his stomach. Consequently, I became alarmed. So did the doctor. We went directly to the hospital from the doctor's office. By the time we got there, I had to get help from an orderly to get Jon from the car to the wheelchair and into admitting. He seemed to be getting weaker by the minute.

As I drove home alone later that day, I had my first vision of life without him. We had no diagnosis, no prognosis. No condition had been identified, no explanations given. Yet, something heavy in the pit of my stomach told me I wouldn't be bringing him back.

When I was in my early twenties, I had watched my grandfather die feeling in touch with something ancient and extremely powerful. The only other time I felt that same sense of awe was when I gave birth. Whether biological or spiritual, the forces in control of life and death are beyond human understanding. Once either birth or death has begun, there is nothing to do but wait and let the body perform what it has been programmed to do for millennia.

The first few days at the hospital, while they were figuring it out, before we knew how very bad it was, before our boy was sent for, he asked me to read *Twelfth Night*, our favorite Shakespearean play. So I read it to him, through nurses coming and going, through the sound of the warm spring rain at the hospital window.

"If music be the food of love, play on.
Give me excess of it, that surfeiting,
The appetite may sicken and so die."

It was the last and best thing we shared, just the two of us. There is no play so full of life, love, and the wonder of human frailty. We clung to every word as though it were scripture, as for us it was. That was to be the sweetest time.

After that, after the diagnosis was finally given, our lives became another kind of drama entirely. Pancreatic cancer has nothing sweet about it. It is the creator of its own inevitable scenario and gives no accommodation to either actors or audience. The best that can be said for it is it is hard, unrelenting, and swift about its business.

For a week we all fought hard, Jon included, to keep life going in that little gray room in the cancer ward. Our son, David, came, as did our most comfortable friend, Ralph, the Victorian Photographer, from Minneapolis. Immediately, they brought music and kept it going. Nobody complained as strains of Chopin, Mozart, and Brahms leaked out onto the hospital floor. Nobody complained

The Place Just Right

about the laughter either. We found dozens of things to laugh about: quirks of the hospital staff, the idiocy of Medicare regulations and the over earnestness of the social workers, the food, spilled cranberry juice, the awkward oxygen mask. Jon's brother came with jokes and memories. We relived many of our own. But most of all, I will remember the phone calls.

MS is an isolating disease, and we had compounded the problem by moving to the Midwest, away from most of Jon's friends and family. I called them all. Day after day for over a week they called him back. Ricky from Paris; Mark from San Francisco; Joe, Konrad, Doug, Bill, from across the country and the world. The cousins and aunts in New York called constantly. It was an amazing outpouring of love and friendship, and it made his last days as joyful as they could be. "This is what it's all about," he said to me, tears in his eyes, as I took the phone from his hands.

As the second week began, he became too weak and confused to respond to the calls. We doubted he could hear us talking, that he was even aware of where he was, of the fact he was dying. Occasionally, he would speak. "You guys are terrific," he said. Another time he looked at me incredulously and said, "This is weird." Once, as David and I were involved in a tense, confusing conversation about where and when we would eat, there came from the bed one of Jon's patented enormous sighs. The kind that came whenever we were being unbelievably ridiculous. It was our last good laugh.

One day near the end he spoke again, so softly I had to lean over to hear the words. It was almost a chant. "*Nycticorax nycticorax.*"

Jon died seventeen days after he entered the hospital. David and I waited as death performed its inevitable, ancient ritual. We sat at the bed and held his hands until we were exhausted, then we each retired to a chair in the dimly lit room and listened to Jon's labored breathing. It was interminable. Finally, I knew it was time. We held him in our arms as his breathing stopped, held him for a long time, poured out our love and grief. Then we held each other. Soon after, I went for the nurse. There was nothing more to do.

Two Thanksgivings

In the *Twilight Zone* episode "Mirror Image," a woman played by Vera Miles waits for a bus in a dingy station, made even dingier by being shot in black and white. Soon, because this is *The Twilight Zone*, peculiar things begin to happen. Her suitcase, not by the wooden bench where she thinks she put it, turns up somewhere else. She begins to catch glimpses of herself from across the station, even on a departing bus. It turns out what she is seeing is, in fact, a doppelgänger, her mythical double or counterpart, who has intruded from an alternate reality and is threatening to take over her life. She is at first helped by a gentleman, played by Martin Milner, who is sympathetic to her situation but who eventually concludes she is insane and turns her over to the men in white coats. Then, of course, he sees his own doppelgänger, and the process begins again.

I have thought frequently of that *Twilight Zone* episode while walking down streets or staring out car windows at the locations where, many decades ago, my life took place. For often I, too, have caught, from the corner of my eye, fleeting glimpses of my own doppelgänger—not a myth from another reality, but a ghost from another time. Once it was my younger self sitting on the steps of the high school in saddle shoes and a crinoline skirt. Another time I saw myself marching across the football field pinging on the glockenspiel, and still another day, strolling down Main Street to Bob's Sweet Shoppe with Jane and Betty Jane. I see my image. I turn to see it better. It isn't really there at all.

Tricks of the mind? Surely not insanity. Probably a spell cast by the imagination with the help of powerful catalysts—place and memory. Maybe even evidence for the contention, found in many philosophies, that time is the real illusion after all, and that all things in the end really do blend into one simultaneous, continuous whole.

The Place Just Right

Nowhere was this experience so startling as in Minneapolis the Thanksgiving after Jon died. Not only did I see myself as I was thirty-five years ago, I seemed to see everyone else from that time as well—in the faces of people in restaurants, through the brightly lit windows of moving streetcars at dusk, in theaters and stores. A veritable crowd of ghosts wearing the same warm jackets and hats, speaking with the usual, wonderful Minnesota inflections. Minneapolis had to have changed in thirty-five years, but the newness appeared to me a thin veneer, a small billboard or flash of neon stuck haphazardly to the old brick buildings still clearly visible and sturdy in their constancy.

Minnesota in late November is already absorbed in winter. Already the weak daylight fades by late afternoon, and rickety wooden steps leading to tiny second-floor apartments are treacherous with patches of ice. Risking splinters, I hold on tightly with both hands on the railings to reach my son's apartment wondering how, laden with bags of groceries, I had ever been so reckless as to rush up my own similar steps in winter so long ago. Jon and I had a landing at the top of our stairs, like my son's, too small ever to be called a porch, the door as it opened outward crowding us back onto the stair steps. Then as now, I teetered even farther back to make room for the dog bounding out to rush down and up again, excited to see somebody after many hours alone.

It is one of the coincidences of our little family that our son, David, was living in Minneapolis during the same years of his life as his father when he lived there. And now I was here too finally, visiting to see where he lived, meeting his roommate, friends, and coworkers, and letting him entertain and provide for me at Thanksgiving instead of the other way round. And not quite so incidentally, time traveling yet again. Feeling the memories wash across the present as water from a sudden storm races in sheets across a low spot in the road. Unable to prevent them even if I had wished them gone.

I was first introduced to Jon by Dr. Nolte shortly after I arrived on the campus of the University of Minnesota. No sparks flew. He looked 1968 scruffy, intense and very young. I came to know his reputation before I knew him. He was perceived as intelligent and talented, but his interests, even in those eclectic days, were off the wall.

He hung around with a small group of friends who were passionate about *Frankenstein*, *Dracula*, and other early Universal Studio's horror movies. They adored *The Twilight Zone*. They had piles of books on vampires, werewolves, and monsters and spent hours watching the movies and reading about the tortured lives of Lon Chaney, Jr., Boris Karloff, and Bela Lugosi. They spoke their own language consisting of quotes from the movies, maniacal sound effects, crazed laughter, and pure nonsense. It was clearly an exclusive little world. I didn't identify with any of it.

I learned about the music and the lizards on the same day. I was asked by my friend Norma Jean to help her with an acting recital, and we needed music behind one of the readings. She called Jon, who came right over with just the right recording, even though, on that day, he was beside himself with guilt and self-loathing. He had brought his pet rainbow lizard, Adrian, outside because there was a patch of sunlight. The lizard had somehow escaped and was gone forever.

Over the next year, we were in a couple of classes and shows together; he was always cast in flamboyant character roles (Lord Byron, a Gypsy) or as a villain or sometimes second lead. He was not a leading man except occasionally in musicals. We nodded at each other politely, but it took what we later referred to as the Robert/Felicia debacle to make us friends.

Robert and Felicia fell passionately in love—a "grand passion" it seemed to us, a precipitous and sudden earth-shattering love of immense proportions—during the course of a production of *The Cherry Orchard* by Chekhov. Robert was a fencing instructor who appeared nineteenth-century Slavic, with a long dour face, lush brown hair and a mustache. He often spoke in a profoundly obtuse way and had about him an intriguing, unflappable military carriage—probably as a result of the fencing. Felicia was a feisty Italian girl, much admired for her courage and intensity onstage, having added to her most recent acting recital an infamous selection from James Joyce, rolling around on pillows on the floor, whispering, "Yes. Yes. Yes."

Nobody made too much of the fact that they fell in love—they were passionate people—except Jon, who was dating Felicia at the time, and me, a recent and obviously short-lived recipient of Robert's amorous attentions. The fact that Robert was married was hardly relevant in 1969; although, it did provide some interesting complications, as it turned out. Since Jon and I were both caught on

The Place Just Right

Jon (and friend) at the University of Minnesota in 1968.

what were, apparently, the losing sides of the same romantic quadrangle, we had our first real conversation. He told me that he, in an attempt to "get to the bottom" of whatever was going on, had asked many questions of Felicia. She told him that his questions were "unanswerable."

Robert's response to Jon's accusatory "Are you sleeping with my girlfriend?" had been even more frustrating.

"What you need to do," he advised Jon, profoundly, "is to reconnoiter."

It didn't take long for Jon's and my first conversation, begun so intensely, to become hilarious. Heartbroken though he was, Jon, I discovered, had an even stronger sense of the ridiculous—a perspective, it turned out, similar to my own. Soon we were topping each other with unflattering, and to us, extremely clever impersonations of Robert and Felicia. It was balm for our bruised egos, of course, but also a revelation to us both that the situation was much less serious than it had seemed. We started hanging around together as things continued to unfold. It was not only companionable; it was also entertaining. It became even more so on Thanksgiving Day.

Before Robert and Felicia fell in love, Robert, in a gesture of largesse, had invited both Jon and me to the home of his in-laws for Thanksgiving dinner. We thought he might rescind the invitation, but, strangely, he didn't. We thought we should probably be considerate and decline to come, but it promised to be a good show, and we figured that as the injured parties, we had every right to watch Robert squirm.

In a fine example of dramatic irony, the family of Herr and Frau Mueller celebrated Thanksgiving totally unaware of the secret lying in wait to change their entire reality. Only Robert knew what we knew. It was clear we made him nervous. Obviously not ready to reveal his new love this day, among these people, he had to be praying that we wouldn't through some hint or chance remark do it for him. Although we did little to reassure him, Jon and I had no intention of forcing his hand. As an audience of two, we were simply there to observe.

Although there was a certain sadness to the situation—especially watching Helga, Robert's blond, flighty wife, openly affectionate with Robert, calling him pet names in her high thin voice—mostly the day was gentle comedy. Frau Mueller cooperated by bustling around frantically, ordering everyone about in an odd mixture of German and English. She appeared at the door: "Pless—to tisch!" she commanded. And when it came time for dessert, a plate suddenly appeared under our noses, and we were commanded, "First—the torte."

"Then the retort," I whispered quietly to Jon, as she moved to the next victim. I knew even by then it was his kind of stupid humor.

~

David, his roommate, Alex, and Alex's girlfriend prepared Thanksgiving dinner in their tiny kitchen. Alex had a recipe for pumpkin soup written in French, sent from Paris by his mother. We had to call another member of his family to be sure we understood what to do. He slipped some foie gras into the dressing. His girlfriend tortured over the gravy. I contributed a potato casserole. We ate around the coffee table for want of a dining room, plates balanced on our laps. It was delicious.

Outside, the weak November daylight faded into evening, and the young people of the neighborhood began to emerge from their small apartments along Lake Calhoun to walk off their Thanksgiving feasts and breathe the brisk air. At the corner of Lake Street and Emerson Avenue, about two blocks from the apartment where I lived in 1969, I saw a couple walking together, winter coats loosely zipped, recklessly braving the evening without hats. Their arms were around each other, and they were laughing as they hurried along, jumping around patches of ice. As they started down Emerson Avenue, I caught a glimpse of their faces. When I turned to see them better, they weren't really there at all.

Ole Man Sorrow

Ole Man Sorrow sittin' by de fireplace,
lyin' all night long by me in de bed.
Tellin'me de same thing mornin', noon an' eb'nin'
that I'm all alone now since my man is dead.
Ah!!!!!!!!!!!!!

"My Man's Gone Now"
Porgy and Bess
Lyrics by DuBose Heyward
Music by George Gershwin

The 1935 opera *Porgy and Bess* did not become a classic by mincing words with human emotion. All the arias cut to the quick, yet for me, none has ever been as affecting as the soaring "My Man's Gone Now." Six months after my husband's death, when it was performed on television in a New Year's Eve special, it reduced me to a puddle. I remember thinking as I excused myself from my hosts and escaped to another room, "What the hell am I supposed to do? I don't think this is ever going to end."

I was right. When I lost my life partner, my soul mate, Ole Man Sorrow moved in to stay. I began to understand that I had to learn to live in spite of him. The only other option was to lie around in a fog of grief for the rest of my days—an image Jon would have detested.

Jon's death had indeed left me "all alone now"—more so than most, it seemed to me. I had no parents, no brothers or sisters. I no longer went to a workplace, and I don't belong to a church. My only child lived far away and had his own life. He commented wryly, "We're a little short on family, aren't we?"

My dearest old friends, and Jon's, were scattered all over the country. Jon and I, dealing with his MS, had not done the usual social things to integrate ourselves into our new Ohio environment. So very soon after Jon's death, I found myself in an empty, echoing house "mornin', noon an' eb'nin'," grizzled Ole Man Sorrow crouching in the spot by the window where Jon's wheelchair had sat.

A uniquely pathetic plight, I thought then. Now I know that even people with extended families, with colleagues at work and a church full of attentive fellow members bringing casseroles, will still not escape the aloneness that comes from the loss of a beloved spouse—even in a room full of well-meaning people. Ole Man Sorrow will move in anyway. Eventually, he has to be confronted head-on.

A few months ago my old high-school buddy Jane lost her husband to cancer. He got to fight a little longer than Jon did, but the result was the same. My heart went out to her. Risking being intrusive, I wrote her a letter. I simply shared my own experience, admitting that hers might be different in some ways. The best comfort I had came from honest letters from friends. Whether Jane was helped or not, writing the letter was immensely useful to me. I began to see how I have come from devastation to a place, if not grief-free, at least more comfortable.

I told Jane that the number of tears in the well to be shed is unbelievable, seemingly inexhaustible, and I would recommend she cry as long and hard as she could, for as many months as she needed, until she was too exhausted to cry anymore. I can't imagine the tension and pain that would result from damming up tears, yet I know some people do. Crying, especially gut-wrenching, gasping spasms of sobbing, must be the body's own way of exorcising emotional distress. Something akin to the way throwing up exorcises toxins from the digestive system. Never mind if it seems childish or embarrassing to scream and howl and roll on the bed clutching a pillow or a stuffed animal. The loss was extreme—the therapy needs to be extreme as well. It is a tremendous relief when it is over. At least until something else triggers the need to cry again. Even so, each episode becomes less prolonged than the one before, so over time a few tears suffice.

Frightened by the feeling that I wanted to do nothing but lie on the couch for the rest of my life, I forced myself to the swimming pool for water exercise the first day I was totally alone. I kept going at least three times a week until the pool closed. Then I started aerobics. I had rarely exercised in the years preceding Jon's death. I was too busy taking care of him.

I told Jane that when I began exercising, I was a dead weight, sluggish and slow to react. But I remembered a concept called "muscle memory" drilled into our heads as acting students years ago. The idea was that creative inspiration and motivation could be activated by going through the physical motions. If, say, the actor were to portray joy, and felt none, skipping, dancing, and putting muscles into the mode of joy could bring about the feeling, eventually. Action and emotion are interconnected so that either one can influence the other. I trusted that to be true. I needed that to be true. So I pressed my body into activity, into the semblance of energy and vitality. I felt as if I were in some symbolic way physically grappling with Ole Man Sorrow. The motivation to get out of bed in the morning slowly came creeping back. Before long, the pool became the best part of my day.

"You have to keep busy. Stay active. Get out of the house." I received this urgent advice from the ladies at the pool, many of whom had also "lost" their husbands. (I always find that phrase disconcerting, as though I had misplaced him somewhere in a crowd. Or left him by mistake at the mall.)

The ladies convinced me that if I didn't stay busy, something dire would happen. I didn't question their collective wisdom. The world is full of widows, and I was grateful to have their experience. I had gone to the pool for the exercise and gotten a support group in the bargain.

Another widowed friend, Nancy T., told me she wouldn't have made it if she hadn't had to go to work. I couldn't do that. When I retired, I had been so overjoyed that going back to teaching was inconceivable, even in my miserable circumstances. So I joined two more women's clubs (in addition to the Alpha Garden Club) and signed up for the Country Kickers line-dancing class. I ran around with Betty Jane and my new friends to movies and restaurants, went shopping and remodeled the house. I attended flower shows and dinner theaters, wherever I was asked. It worked for a while. I met new people, and time passed. But the couch still called, even more seductively than it had during the first terrible week, and I began to think being alone and totally passive for a while might not be so frightening. In fact, it might be welcome.

The Place Just Right

I talked about it with my son. "Do what makes you feel good, Mom," he said. From the sense of relief I felt when he gave me permission, I knew his was good advice as well. I had reached a stage where I needed large doses of laziness and self-indulgence. I told Jane this particular self-pampering period lasted a couple of months. I learned to say "No thanks" to most of the activities and indulged in all the guilty, mindless pleasures people hide from each other.

I made it a priority to watch *The Young and the Restless* every day live—not taped—on my new big-screen TV. (Many new widows report buying something terribly expensive after their husbands die. I don't know if men do it also.) I read dozens of trashy novels. I spent hours at the computer playing various kinds of solitaire. I watched the US Open tennis tournament obsessively from the earliest matches through the finals. Had it not been for walking the dog and the exercise class, I believe I would have spent many days without leaving the house. I regressed to adolescence, if not quite childhood.

Between my escapes into trivia, I still cried, stumbling over Ole Man Sorrow lurking in various spots in the house, but it wasn't long before a peculiar sort of satisfying relaxation began to emerge. In spite of myself, I found I was warming to the idea that I no longer had any obligations to anyone but myself. I was not a teacher; I was not a daughter; I didn't need to earn money or actively mother my son. I didn't have to take care of anybody at all, except the dog. Furthermore, I didn't need to be efficient, capable, cultured, talented, or even very intelligent.

Well-meaning people said to me after Jon died, "Now you are free," referring, of course, to my years of coping with Jon's MS. I didn't understand what they meant. I found the remark insensitive. I adored him. Coping with his illness was a small price to pay to have him around.

I replied bitterly with a phrase from an old song, "Freedom's just another word for nothing left to lose."

Now, for the first time, curled up on my couch, listening to the Dixie Chicks, I began to discover another side to being alone. I could see it as liberation, not just from caretaking, but from Jon's influence in everything from TV and music to food and home decorating. After thirty years and all the adjustments and compromises considerate marriage partners make, I had begun to think our tastes and interests were nearly inseparable. We had shared all those things so closely;

Brenda Baumhart Mezz

I had to reach back indeed to adolescence to find something I would not have done together with him. Except for watching *The Young and the Restless*, which after Jon became housebound was a guilty pleasure for both of us, I realized I had been doing things I would have felt uncomfortable doing when he was around. From somewhere an independent me was struggling to be born.

I didn't share all that with Jane. She will have to discover her own independent person. I hope it won't take her as long as it is taking me. Nearing the third anniversary of Jon's death, I am still struggling to be born—still swinging between too much activity and too little, between frittering away my time and filling my calendar so full I'm barely ever home. But it's getting better all the time.

The other day I glanced over to the spot by the window where Jon's wheelchair used to sit. Ole Man Sorrow was crouched there as usual looking at me quizzically. I stared at him defiantly and squared my shoulders, and as I did a mist formed over his features. For just a second, Jon's face appeared. He was smiling at me, nodding approval. When the mist cleared and Ole Man Sorrow's aged visage returned, he was nodding, too. I know he will never leave. But he is becoming better company.

Pollywog

It takes less than a second to recognize her on the phone.

"Hi, honey," she sings, her voice balancing delicately on the upper end of the scale. "It's Pollywog." Then she laughs. A birdsong giggle, a trill playing hopscotch along the branches of the higher registers.

"Hi, Polly," I reply. We make plans for lunch.

Polly is flighty about where she likes to eat. At first we went to the Country Club. Lately, she likes the Chinese place in the Kroger plaza among the office and construction workers on break, or what she calls the "Eaton, Eaton, Eaton, Eaton Place," a huge buffet in Richmond. Recently, we drove up to the interstate to a travelers/truck stop to try out its buffet. At ninety-three, Polly has lost none of her appetite—for food, or adventure.

Wherever we go, Polly strikes up conversations with perfect strangers. Generally, they love it. Although she looks slightly eccentric in her loose black pants, long shirts or sweaters, jewelry, and occasional hats, she is definitely non-threatening, honestly cheerful, and interested in the people she sees. Sometimes, she gets recognized. People will approach her.

Polly was once a reporter for a Dayton newspaper—still writes a weekly column for the Eaton paper, serves on civic committees, gives speeches, works with troubled kids. People are grateful. They smile, pat her on the shoulder, give her compliments. They leave thinking they have greeted a lively nonagenarian who has some reputation in this town. They have no inkling they have been talking to a prophet who knows the secrets to the forces of the universe and the meaning of life.

Pollywog is the mother of one of my closest friends from high school, a friend Jon nicknamed "the Arbiter" because she once sent us an article from the company newsletter of a very large corporation with a picture of herself behind her desk. She had been promoted to "Chief Knowledge Officer," according to the article. Jon, always a joker, told me to ask her if that meant she was the arbiter of all knowledge. "Something like that," she answered. So "the Arbiter" she remained.

Of course, she was joking, too, although before she retired she was in the vanguard of those people able to instruct their computers to predict the future by following trends and making projections. She seemed to have an instinct for it. But, unlike her mother, she will not be tied down about the secrets of the universe.

The Arbiter, who doesn't live in Eaton, asked me please to keep an eye on Pollywog. Now, I consider Polly a friend in her own right, even though she does make me squirm by forcing me to examine my own beliefs about the meaning of life as she confidently shares the details of her own.

The farther I have moved from urban centers and cosmopolitan people, the more often I have encountered individuals who are convinced they have the answer to all the great mysteries. In Los Angeles, within a few miles of the neighborhoods where I once resided, are Jewish, Buddhist, and Hindu temples, Greek Orthodox and Roman Catholic cathedrals, Muslim mosques, and every variety of church or study group imaginable, from gurus, Scientologists, psychics, and other California eccentrics to the most traditional mainstream Baptists. Within earshot of the din of all those messages at once, it was hard to believe any one of them had the inside track to the truth. Most people I knew were more than willing to accept that their way to enlightenment, assuming they had found or were born into one, was not the only way.

Here in Eaton and throughout the heartland, traditional Christianity rules. Anything else is suspiciously exotic. "We pray that Osama bin Laden comes to know Jesus," intoned the new chaplain of the Alpha Garden Club at the first meeting after 9/11, as though Osama bin Laden were a pagan needing to be saved. Never mind that the ferocity of Osama bin Laden's own religious convictions fed his actions and those of other terrorists in the first place. Such fervor of

The Place Just Right

belief, such certainty of faith, has created havoc for centuries, and Christianity has its own dubious history in the cultivation of murderous fanatics. The Salem witch trials are only one example.

Not that I find religious fanatics around every corner in the Midwest—just a world almost uniformly Christian. Given my life's journey up to this point, this is a strange experience for me.

When Jon was dying in the hospital, the kindly Quaker chaplain implored me, "Tell me what I can do for you."

"Find me a rabbi," I said. I desperately wanted Jon in his final days to hear the familiar Hebrew prayers from his childhood. The chaplain tried but couldn't help me. There were no rabbis to be found in Richmond, Indiana. For the first and possibly the only time, I cursed ever having moved back to the Midwest.

A few days later, the kindly Quaker chaplain approached me again, as though I really hadn't heard him the first time. "Tell me what I can do for you." This time I understood he wasn't talking about what Jon's spirit needed—he was talking about what my spirit needed.

"Nothing," I replied. "Thank you for your concern." He left us alone.

It was one of the few times I have ever envied those who derive solace from prayer and faith. It must feel like I felt as a child nestled into the soft lap of my adored grandmother Frances, relaxing against her shoulder, smelling her lavender soap. Nothing could hurt me then.

Unfortunately, I grew out of the faith I was taught as a child, and am neither old enough nor battered enough to return to those innocent ideas, even in terrible times when it would feel so very reassuring. Climbing into the lap of Jesus feels to me like climbing into the lap of a cloud. If for one second I doubted its substance, it would dissolve, leaving me to drift aimlessly in open space. Faith, like imagination, appears to be beautiful, joyous, miraculous—but in my experience, insubstantial. My faith flew immediately in the face of doubt and skepticism. I was born skeptical. Ultimately, I prefer it that way. Even in terrible times.

The Quakers, ever gracious, refer to people in my position as "seekers." They value that status, unlike some religious traditions that view skeptics with pity and condescension. Or worse. I was bemused by that term when I first became aware of it, presuming it was a euphemism for something less complimentary. Now I like it, because it is exactly what I aspire to be—a seeker. Like the Pollywog.

What Polly and I have in common in Eaton is that neither one of us is comfortable with traditional Christian answers. We are compelled to discover things for ourselves. The difference between Polly and me is that Polly has been seeking the ultimate truth constantly and intensely, while I have only pondered the eternal questions idly, now and then, when they are brought to my attention. Consequently, she has produced results in the form of a system of belief that is all her own—hers and those of a few dozen other people I occasionally find in her living room when I drop by unannounced. Her study group. I have no results. The more I learn, the less I know—as the old maxim goes.

There are other differences as well. Polly has psychic and mystical powers. Her search began more than fifty years ago with a vision that reached into the very core of the life force—the perception of a luminosity emanating from all things, animate and inanimate. A luminosity not unlike that described in certain experiences of mystics that I have encountered in literature and theology. My own mystic visions have been few and far between, and I am embarrassed to admit, the result of two LSD trips I took in the sixties. None of these perceptions were particularly insightful, although they did give me an example as to how such things might occur—with or without the use of hallucinogens.

If I am too skeptical to be traditional, I am certainly too skeptical to become a disciple of the Pollywog, although I think her study group must be a lot more fun than Bible Study. I also admire the joy and health Polly's vision of the cosmos has brought her in her very long life. For her, common plants glow with vitality, trees dance with the antics of spirits, and walls carry messages in the contrasting colors of their bricks. My own search is much more passive than is Polly's. I've read enough books on the subject to be thoroughly confused. Reading scripture pales next to reading Shakespeare, and any time I have prayed, I feel stupid because I detect no response at all. So I sit quietly, and I listen like Siddhartha "with a waiting, open soul, without passion, without desire, without judgments, without opinions." And I watch for signs.

The Place Just Right

Two days before Jon died, in the late afternoon, I was coming home from the hospital for a short rest before continuing the bedside vigil that evening. Our dear friend Ralph, the Victorian Photographer, was driving, and it was raining as it had been most of the week. Suddenly, the sun appeared through the still-falling rain, and I said to him, "There has to be a rainbow here somewhere."

I looked to my left and saw it forming along the edge of some dark gray clouds. Ralph pulled off the road into the parking lot of the tiny art center on the southern edge of Eaton, and we watched as the rainbow brightened and extended across the entire eastern sky. Then to our surprise, as we sat there, a second rainbow took shape under the first, its smaller arch forming what looked for all the world like a luminous passage into heaven. We both had the same reaction—a passage opening for Jon from this life to the next.

A few weeks later, I took Polly to lunch. "I located him," she said.

"Who?" I asked. "Located who?"

"Jon. He's in one of the most beautiful places of all, and he's going to be someone very important."

I cleared my throat, and blurted out awkwardly. "Uh—well, how is he?"

Polly smiled at me. "Whole. He's whole," she said.

At that moment, I believed her without a single doubt.

Tellin' Me I'm Ole Now

> *Ole Man Sorrow's marchin' all de way wid me,*
> *Tellin' me I'm ole now*
> *Since I lose my man.*
> PORGY AND BESS

I always supposed it happened the other way around. First a woman got old. Then she lost her man. But after my husband died, when I heard again "My Man's Gone Now," I felt I had discovered a forgotten truth—I wasn't really old while my husband was alive. Suddenly, after he was gone, I was.

I have read stories of people whose hair turned white overnight due to some terrible shock or loss. My sudden aging with the onset of widowhood was nothing that dramatic, but a passage nonetheless. I simply found myself in a totally different world, one I had been aware was there and inhabited by other human beings, just not by me.

I realized, for instance, I was supposed to be taking personally all the jokes about sagging bodies, failing memories, and sexual malfunction that flooded in over the Internet. I got invited to the Red Hat Society which celebrates eccentric older ladies who, because they are past caring, can now wear and do what they like. AARP discovered me, as did Medicare, and I began to get buckets of mail about long-term care, supplemental health insurance, and preplanned funerals. Going out to dinner, I found I was automatically credited with the senior discount. This must be the insult at the other end of life that complements the insult of being carded in a bar at the age of twenty-one.

The marketers of the modern American economy have apparently decided just what sort of world older people should inhabit. In the company of the "ladies," I often imagine I am visiting a theme park designed just for elders with cafeterias and family restaurants serving cheap, early meals; dinner theaters showing fare at least fifty years old; bus trips to gardens, flower shows, and concerts by Wayne Newton; and department stores filled with comfortably oversize dresses, "relaxed" pants, and sensible shoes.

For a while I treated it as a novelty, scanning the scene with detached amusement, remarking on the peculiarities of all the denizens of this funny little subculture. Then I realized if I was not yet one of them, indistinguishable from the rest, I soon would be. I was clearly perceived as one of them by waitresses, clerks, bus drivers, and all the other securely young people who assisted and patronized their elders in this theme park. Quietly passing my tray along the MCL Cafeteria line, selecting the overcooked roast beef and limp green beans, I have more than once experienced a moment of panic, shouting inside, "Somebody, please. Get me out of here!"

Of course, there is no rescue from getting old. But some handle it more gracefully than others. The golden years are touted by marketers as a period of relaxation, freedom from responsibility, and a time to indulge long-postponed pleasures and adventures. However, I am finding as I watch the people I meet, it is hard work to be old. Especially for people who are alone. My mother-in-law, Dotty, spent her last years living by herself in an apartment in Manhattan. For most of those years, whenever anyone would ask her how she was, she would reply, "I'm vertical." We laughed, as did she. But it also communicated her perception of the will required to keep going—to remain standing tall when each day demanded a little more effort than the previous day to rise to her feet and go out the door into the New York streets.

I have been treated here in Eaton to dozens of models for growing old, some so graceful and admirable I almost feel happy to become a senior citizen. Virginia from my exercise classes, in her eighties, moves through the exercises faster than anybody and is always rushing off to one of the dozens of activities that fill her days. Her spirit is inspiring and her laughter infectious. Several of the women from the Alpha Garden Club seem to have grown only sweeter with age, glowing with sensitivity, inner strength, and wisdom. Would that all the widows I meet were like them. There are, unfortunately, plenty of others who provide much less encouraging examples.

Not too long ago I encountered a woman in my neighborhood. I had noticed a FOR SALE sign in her yard. "Why are you leaving? You just got here," I said. She told me her story.

She is a widow—three years now. She had been blessed for forty years, she told me, to be married to the most wonderful husband in the world. She still cried for him every day. She had moved to Lakengren to be near a daughter and grandchildren but had discovered immediately that the house was too much. She had been terrified by the ice in the driveway in winter, hadn't made friends, and was afraid to drive into Eaton in the dark. She was depressed and fragile, though I could see she wasn't much older than I am. She told me she was planning to move into the apartments in the new senior community on the northern edge of Eaton—the ones in the same compound as the assisted-living facility, which is, in turn, attached to the nursing home. I shuddered. They are lovely apartments, to be sure—very modern and clean. But it felt like capitulation to me.

I felt guilty. I hadn't been neighborly enough to go knock on her door. Then, I got defensive. She hadn't knocked on my door either or inquired about activities in Lakengren. Many widows, I find, are very timid. They are unused to doing anything alone. If something seems even the least bit challenging, they back off. If there is one thing I have learned in the years I have been a widow, it is that timidity doesn't work. Nobody is likely to walk up the driveway and knock on the door, although in Lakengren there is supposed to be a welcoming committee. Headed by Virginia, as a matter of fact. I'll have to call it to her attention. This lady fell through the cracks, somehow.

It is too easy to imagine crowds of old people falling through the cracks every day. Seniors alone, floundering, wondering how they got into such a predicament, where the years went. How all their friends, family, and support systems could have disappeared. Old age is truly "not for sissies." It carries with it some really nasty problems. Each one of them requires energy, spunk, and aggressiveness. Sadly, those are the very qualities that tend to dwindle with age.

The Place Just Right

My Aunt Ruth and Uncle Buzz reported to me recently on the death of a gentleman we all knew. I asked how the widow was doing. Ruth shook her head. "She's helpless," she said. "Her children are doing everything for her. She doesn't drive. She never balanced a checkbook. She doesn't know how much money she has or what to do with it. He did it all." I used to hear this a lot growing up. The male ego, in the days before the feminist movement, ran wild with control of every practical or monetary issue in the household, and women let it happen, gratefully relinquishing the worldly decisions to their big, strong men—with the sad result that they were helpless when the men were rude enough to die first and leave it all in their soft but flabby little hands.

I feel terrible about this lady, but also a little irritated. Dotty was in the same situation when Jon's father, Irving, died. His hobby in retirement had been to play little games with his investments. He had stocks, bonds, mutual funds, and IRAs scattered all over, each maturing at different times, some taxable, some not—a true labyrinth of confusion. But Dotty, at eighty, with a little initial help from us, buckled down and got a handle on it. She bombarded dozens of clerks, brokers, and insurance agents with questions, made copious lists of phone numbers, addresses, and due dates, entered everything into account books, and made it something she could do. She didn't do it without some teeth gnashing, cursing, and complaining, but she did it. Nobody ever accused Dotty of being timid.

I am determined to follow her example. Unless and until my mind is incapacitated with dementia (the only situation I can imagine that could render me totally helpless), I intend to hold my ground. I will not capitulate anything without a fight. I know that's what it will take. I can spot the enemy just over the horizon creeping up on me in the shadows, preparing its arsenal. I'm getting ready. I am already constructing my widow's resolutions.

I resolve to get off my duff and out the door.

I resolve to watch my diet, keep buying makeup, and wearing new clothes in the youngest styles I can without looking ridiculous.

I resolve to set challenges and pursue their completion knowing that if I lose my motivation to achieve something new, something hard, I might also lose my motivation to keep living.

I resolve to live in my house until I am so demented, they have to drag me out of it kicking and screaming. I will consort with other old ladies because I like them, but I will also see to it that I get around young people as well to keep my attitude up-to-date.

I resolve to hold on to my personhood, remembering that within a changing body, I am the same girl I was growing up in Eaton; the same woman who once could make an audience laugh or cry, and who successfully taught gang members to read Shakespeare. I resolve to keep alive her curiosity, her ability to laugh and love, and her anticipation of the sun coming up in the morning.

Growing old is the last challenge. I always assumed I would be facing it together with Jon, hand in hand. Instead, I got Ole Man Sorrow "marchin all de way wid me." Still—the lesson of loss is that life is precious. That lesson is a gift to me from Jon's death. I resolve to learn it well.

Jon would expect nothing less.

***

The writer and media personality Heywood Hale Broun died a number of years ago. In the flattering obituaries aired about his life, he was reported to have said the following (paraphrased liberally): "When the end of one's life approaches, and most of the goals, passions, and activities that used to be important are over, what remains is curiosity."

I can already affirm this is true. At least for me. I am developing great confidence of late in the power of curiosity. I fully expect curiosity to be my life jacket thrown into the pool, my alarm clock in the morning, and the substance of my last thoughts of the evening before drifting off to sleep. Following the path of curiosity will, in all probability, provide me the most adventure, and at its end, the most satisfaction to be found in the years to come. It can, as long as my mind remains sound, outlast husbands, lovers, and friends, and provide the best kind of solace for their loss as the years wind down. It is already working its magic.

What is there to be curious about? Why, that's the beauty of it. A limitless number of things, almost anything, in fact, in the entire world. Steve Hartman is a CBS broadcast journalist. (I first saw him in Los Angeles, then nationally).

The Place Just Right

He used to move about the country filming a series called *Everybody Has a Story*. He, or somebody whose life he has just covered, stands in front of a map of the United States with his or her back turned and throws a dart over his or her shoulder. Wherever it lands is the town Hartman visits. Once there, he opens the phone book at random, and with his eyes closed points to a name. That is the person whose story he tells. He always finds something interesting, no matter who it is.

That is the joy of curiosity. Wherever it is pointed, whether at trees, buildings, birds, politics, or the sky itself—there is always some path to follow. And once someone starts down that path—wherever it is—the excitement only increases. With curiosity, the more one learns, the more there is to learn. Every answer creates another question. Soon, there isn't enough time in the day to search out all the information or follow all the paths that come into view.

I love it when I see somebody (usually, but not always, a retired somebody) who adores lighthouses, bottle caps or stuffed bears, movie posters or antiques. I love the eccentrics with basements full of toy trains, pictures of clowns, or Elvis memorabilia. They are experts in whatever it is they love—masters of the arcane, the details of their piece of history, or the world of knowledge. And I absolutely worship naturalists who study the behavior of the tiniest insects, or history buffs who visit every site of some war and read every scrap they can about a certain corner of time or place.

I aspire to become an archivist of some field of study—to know more about *something* than anybody else in the world, like my new acquaintance, Orville, archivist of the Amherst Historical Society in Amherst, Ohio, who painstakingly catalogues the names of the family members of the earliest settlers of Lorain County. Never mind that only a handful of other people either know or care about that particular thing. When Orville and I met on the phone the other day, and he answered my question with delicious detail, we were both as animated and involved as two teenagers talking about their dates for the prom. Now, how else could two people, one sort of old (me), the other even older (I think), get that kind of excitement out of life?

For my own journey down the pathways that curiosity carves, I have discovered the map of my own genealogy. Almost any starting place would have done just as well. As a teacher I was always intrigued by the concept of branch learning. Now, as a student again, I am as free as a squirrel to turn down any branch of knowledge and sit there for as long as I like. The darts I have thrown at the map of my genealogy have landed, among other places, on the Protestant Reformation, in Switzerland with Zwingli, on slave galleys where Anabaptists were sent as punishment for their beliefs, on the encroachment of barbarian tribes at the edges of the Roman Empire, on immigration and the earliest events of American history and the opening up of the Northwest Territory. The list could go on and on—and most certainly will. It is already including, beyond history: economics, genetics, invention, religion, pacifism, linguistics, and agriculture.

I always wondered what all those self-absorbed people saw in tracing their family tree, besides possibly finding hidden royalty or a lost family treasure. Now I know. Some of everyone's ancestors have been there for most of the major events of the world.

Once while looking at family trees offered by one website or another, I found one that included Cleopatra, Ivan the Terrible, Charlemagne, King Arthur, Marco Polo, Julius Caesar, and most of the great and famous figures of history. It was obviously someone's idea of a joke—and I thought it was very funny. But it also had an element of truth. Somewhere in the mists of ancient evolution, we are indeed all related. Getting closer to that concept could go a long way toward solving many of our problems.

One more unexpected benefit of curiosity.

Family

A gathering of aunts, uncles, and cousins.

Cousin Sarah always comes home to Eaton for the Famous Preble County Fair. The fair is truly famous, of course, only to the forty-five thousand or so residents of Preble County. Nevertheless, as long as I can remember, the word is a necessary part of the name—even as officially printed in the *Register-Herald*. "The Famous Preble County Fair." Nobody finds it the least bit ironic.

Brenda Baumhart Mezz

Although Sarah is now a successful attorney in Florida, and has certainly been to Busch Gardens and Disney World and other *really* famous attractions, she has a soft spot in her heart for the local fair. To my knowledge, she hasn't missed a year, even though, like me until I moved back, she hasn't lived in Eaton for a very long time. The fair was an important part of life for her side of the family.

Aunt Ruth and Uncle Buzz lived in the country and farmed. They showed horses at the fair. Small horses. Ponies, maybe. There are pictures of little Sarah looking cute as a button in white ruffles, seated in a beribboned miniature carriage hitched to a gussied-up pony. It was a big deal. Buzz was even a member of the fair board for years—responsible for being the first to bring a major country music star to head the bill at the grandstand for the main show.

Now Sarah brings her children home for the fair. In fact, they come a week or more before she does to stay with Ruth and Buzz or with cousin Rodger and his kids in order to spend time with their cousins and get a taste of small-town life. This year her oldest boy begged off for the first time, apparently having something more exciting to do in the city, but the other two, says Sarah, show entirely new and wonderful facets of their personalities in Eaton. They play. They relax. They laugh. It is hard to be around Uncle Buzz for long without laughing. Whether you are a child or an adult, he will tease you unmercifully until you do. I remember that vividly from growing up around him. There is nothing like some affectionate teasing to make overwrought preadolescent horrors seem normal and laughable, embarrassing though it might be at the time.

When Sarah comes home, the family gathers for a little "do." Since I have been back, I get invited. I get to go as well to the early Thanksgiving celebrations held at either Rodger's or Cousin Steve's in Cincinnati. These dinners are full-scale Thanksgiving feasts eaten prior to Thanksgiving because Ruth and Buzz are snowbirds. Like many Ohio residents, they spend the winter in Florida, in their case, St. Petersburg, near Sarah. It's a close family and growing as it should. Ruth and Buzz have three children, nine grandchildren, and now, two chubby, feisty, gorgeous great-granddaughters, the offspring of Steve's oldest daughter.

A "do" with Ruth and Buzz and family is about as casual as such things can be. The house in town where they now live isn't quite as spacious as the old farm,

The Place Just Right

but with the added-on room and screened-in porch, and with the kids spilling out onto the ample lawn, there is plenty of space. The porch holds a table for the kids and one for the adults, and the grilled hot dogs and steaks, steaming corn on the cob, baked beans, and potato casserole fit nicely on the sideboard between the kitchen and the living room.

Everybody pitches in: Steve and Rodger at the grill, Patti and Karen (their respective wives) setting things out and keeping track of the kids, Ruthie in charge of the pot of boiling sweet corn, Sarah the contributor of two magnificent key lime pies. It works like a well-practiced, comfortable dance. The kind of rhythmic movement that, I suppose, develops in most families over time. The kind of domestic comfort and predictability that is taken for granted. Not, however, taken for granted by me.

Since I, the prodigal relative, have returned to this town, I have been struggling to understand what my role should be among these people. Forty years is a very long time to be away and, except for an occasional sighting of Sarah when my mother lived in Florida, out of touch. The young adults I knew are now patriarch and matriarch, the children—adults. There are wives and new children whom I am only now learning to know. What can I expect from them? What should they expect of me?

I look around the room at this family and remember Jon's shocked reaction when, at the first of such gatherings we attended, Ryan, Rodger's oldest, and in his teens, announced to Buzz with pride, "Grandpa, I made the honor roll!" He was so fresh faced, clean-cut, and all-American looking, as indeed were the rest of them, that Jon, the New Yorker, thought he had walked into a Norman Rockwell painting. Neither of us realized that Midwestern families could still look like that and not consider themselves a cliché. That as the rest of the world became savvy, sophisticated, and cynical, honest wholesomeness could still be found in all its un-self-conscious innocence.

At the recent gathering to welcome Sarah on her yearly visit during the fair, several trays of old slides had been retrieved from somewhere and laid on the coffee table. Sarah had been going through them trying to decide how to bring them into the modern age so they might be enjoyed again. Through a clumsy viewer against an unshaded lightbulb, I studied the slides she handed me.

Brenda Baumhart Mezz

"Remember this? Oh, look at your mom in that dress! There's Lucy, the Wonder Dog. Is that Cousin Ben or Dan? I can't tell."

The pictures jolted me like little thrills of electricity. They were not pictures I had ever seen before. Not the same ones that had made it into my own scrapbooks at home. They were pictures of this family, and my mother and I were all over them. There was Helyn standing over a Thanksgiving turkey on a long table laid in our house on Richmond Pike. There was our incredible dog, Lucy, begging a piece of turkey from Judge Burke, Mother's companion for years and a huge person in my life. He was obviously important to this family as well.

Grandma Nina was there and Arleene from the Garber farm. There was a picture of me and my friend Nancy T., from the trip to Italy, with Cousin Steve riding along looking important as we left to meet the ship in New York. I was there in a hospital bed the summer before my sophomore year in college when I had a little surgery. And finally, best of all, me at nineteen, sitting tall in the middle—six little faces, five to twelve years old, looking up at me—the cool older cousin who got to have all the adventures first.

Sarah leaned in closer to look with me through the viewer, un-self-consciously, like a sister, arm across my shoulder.

When I left, I said to Buzz, "Thank you so much for including me."

A puzzled look crossed his face. "Why are you thanking me?" he said. "You're family." I smiled all the way home.

BJ and the Baptists

*B*etty Jane called about noon to confirm our Sunday night dinner out. She was unusually insistent about the time and place. "I want to be at Frisch's at 7:00," she said. "So you should be here by 6:50 at the latest."

"Okay," I replied. I didn't give her an argument. Her assertive tone took me back to our high-school days when she had been an in-charge young lady—proud, popular, and sure of herself. Lately, I had been catching glimpses of that again. I hoped it was a sign she was finally regaining some self-confidence after years of feeling depressed and overwhelmed at finding herself an unwilling divorcée.

Betty Jane and I had begun hanging out on the weekends. Eaton is a family community. Widows and divorcées who are sixty plus, like us, don't have many social options, especially if their children are busy, disinterested, or live in other states. Therefore, we started making plans with each other for Friday, Saturday, and Sunday nights. We often went to Dayton or Richmond, but Betty Jane wanted to stay in Eaton on Sunday. She has to be at work at the doctor's office early on Monday mornings.

Everyone here knows the choices for dining in Eaton are pathetic. My aunt Ruth reminds me that this town once boasted several wonderful restaurants. People even came from Dayton to eat here. Now there is nothing except fast-food drive-ins, Frisch's and McCabe's Pub. McCabe's Pub is a more convivial place, but the mostly grilled menu gets old very quickly. Frisch's is a family restaurant. The menu is full of traditional, dull Midwestern entrees with mounds of potatoes and gravy, but it has a tolerable salad bar and fairly good vegetable soup.

Brenda Baumhart Mezz

When Betty Jane and I arrived at Frisch's, promptly at 7:00, she was still managing things. She selected a booth with a window to the parking lot and seated herself facing the restaurant entrance, in which she seemed to be taking great interest. Her eyes kept darting in that direction. We ordered our food. It had barely arrived when she suddenly stiffened and said, urgently, "Don't turn around!" Startled, I immediately turned around. She hissed something at me, and I reluctantly turned back. But I kept sneaking peeks, as did she from under her hands that were partially covering her eyes.

I couldn't imagine what could be happening in Frisch's Big Boy restaurant in Eaton on Sunday night that could be this dramatic. All I could see in my furtive glimpses was a group of about twenty-five people of assorted ages, dressed for Sunday-go-to-meetin', standing just past the entrance looking startled and indecisive. They were staring at our table. After a few minutes of utter confusion, a portly man in white shirt and tie began herding the crowd back toward the entrance and out the door, even pulling with them a few of the younger ones who had already sat in the booths. We could see them through the window hurrying to their cars and driving away.

I looked at Betty Jane. She had a smug grin on her face. "You sure know how to clear a room," I said. "What the hell is going on?" Betty Jane, it turned out, had just scored a victory over her ex-husband and the Baptists.

A little local lore.

Since World War I, but especially after World War II, an enormous migration of people from Appalachia drifted north seeking work. The new immigrants were poor, their customs and accents different, and many were or became evangelical Baptists. Although most headed for factories in nearby small cities, some drifted into rural Preble County—among them the large family of strapping, basketball-playing boys into which my friend Betty Jane married. This particular family became infamous for its rapid integration through marriage into the traditional social fabric of an otherwise staid, standoffish town. Betty Jane's parents fought the relationship tooth and nail—and lost the battle. Did I mention she was headstrong in those days?

More accommodating was the editor of the local newspaper, whose daughter married into the same large family. For almost fifty years, from his newspaper

The Place Just Right

office, and later from the retirement home, he published every visit, every birthday party, every new job of this family in veritably all of his weekly newspaper columns—much to the exasperated amusement of the generation of readers who saw a great deal of irony in the resulting local celebrity of these upstarts.

A year or so after Betty Jane married and much to her surprise, her husband and one of his brothers got the call to the Baptist ministry. She followed her man into the life of the church. They were called to several places around the country. She learned to play the piano, lead the choir, and perform all the duties of a pastor's wife. At the last church and after forty years of marriage and six daughters, it all came to an end when Betty Jane's Baptist minister husband was seen too often in the company of a woman from the congregation. He lost his job as well as his wife, the resulting disruption throwing both of their lives and those of their children into disarray. Betty Jane, after a few confusing years, quietly returned home, expecting to make a new life.

It wasn't a month until her expectations were shattered. Her ex-husband, in a masterful stroke of bad timing, also returned to Eaton. He made no quiet entrance. He and his brother advertised the opening of a new church. His large family of brothers and sisters formed the core, in fact, the entire congregation. He resumed communication with his daughters, shutting Betty Jane out of holidays and other celebrations. But worst of all, "she" was constantly present at his side, "she," the woman who had ruined Betty Jane's life in the first place. "She" began showing up with him at high-school athletic events where the grandchildren participated and at Frisch's with the family/congregation on Sunday night after services.

It was for Betty Jane an embarrassing, humiliating, and, most of all, profoundly depressing situation. For a long time she had been at a loss as to what to do about it. Now—she had finally found something that worked. She had staked out her very own territory at Frisch's, denying that crowd, by her sheer unmovable presence, at least one space in this town. A generation of Eatonians would have cheered on her behalf had they seen the confusion as the congregation/family scrambled for their cars.

On the following Sunday night we were back at Frisch's promptly at 7:00. This time Betty Jane chose a booth with a view of the outdoor sidewalk leading to the entrance of the building. The venetian blind at the window was partially closed, a space perhaps a foot tall open at the bottom. We ordered our food. It had barely arrived when Betty Jane, whose eyes had been darting out the window, suddenly sat up very straight and burst out laughing. "What's going on?" I asked.

"They're here. And they're leaving again," she announced. I parted the venetian blind and was treated to the sight of parking cars being intercepted, hurried consultations through rolled-down windows, arms waving, and then multiple departures as the cars pulled out onto Barron Street and sped away. "How...?" I started to ask.

"It was a kid," she answered. "Her kid. They sent him ahead. He peeked through the window, our window as it turned out, and stared me straight in the face. I wish you could have seen the look he gave me." She laughed over it for most of our meal.

On the third Sunday, they pulled into the parking lot, parked, evidently determined we were there, and walked down the street to Kentucky Fried Chicken. When we finished eating, we hung out for a while in the parking lot at Pizza Hut across the street to count their cars as they left and ascertain that "she" was riding with the ex-husband. It seemed important to Betty Jane to know that.

On the fourth and fifth Sundays, they didn't come at all. We both felt cheated. Sunday night in Eaton was becoming far too dull. Besides, we were dying of curiosity. Where had they decided to eat, and would we dare, if we found out, start accidentally showing up there as well—promptly at 7:00? We daydreamed about that.

The next Sunday I picked up Betty Jane at 6:40, and we drove a circuitous route to the area of the church, parking along an adjacent street where we could see the cars leaving the church parking lot and where, hopefully, they wouldn't see us. Betty Jane dropped down in her seat. It wasn't long before the cars began to leave, turning north a block away. We headed north up a parallel street hoping to keep them in our sight at the intersections. It worked fine for a few blocks, and then we lost them. "Turn left," Betty Jane ordered. Bad decision. We came face-to-face with the ex-husband's car.

"Duck!" I yelled, and she headed for the floor.

The Place Just Right

I guess they never knew. At least we heard nothing about it. We killed a little time and then headed north, up Barron Street, hoping to discover the cars somewhere in the direction they were headed. We finally saw them at Arby's on the northern edge of town and drove around the building to count heads and see if "she" was along.

Apparently, they didn't like Arby's much, because they never went back. We made desultory stabs at locating them on a few occasions. After all, there isn't much choice in Eaton, and they would hardly be expected to appear at McCabe's Pub. Finally, Betty Jane figured they were having a potluck at the church. She would have made a wonderful private investigator because her insight was absolutely right. This foray we timed perfectly, passing by the church at precisely 7:35. I saw them on the first pass, through a glass door, sitting at a long paper-topped table hunched over their plates. Betty Jane missed it, so we risked coming around again.

Sadly, there wasn't much we could do after that. There was no way to chase them from their own church. So we gave it up and resigned ourselves to the usual end-of-the-week conversations—how work went, how my projects were coming along, whether or not Betty Jane might, after all, be better off in Florida. Did she really have the courage to pick up and go?

While she makes that decision, we still meet at Frisch's and talk about our adventure—two sad, lonely senior citizens chasing around in the car, acting like teenagers all over again, up to no good, getting even. It's great therapy. I recommend it. No use acting your age, we decide. Life is way too short.

The Alpha Garden Club Christmas Meeting

Route 122, west out of Eaton, passes through a lovely section of town. Near the very edge of the city limits, across from historic Mound Hill Cemetery and not far from the entrance to Fort St. Clair, sprawls the Lutheran church. Behind that, along Lutheran Drive, is a neighborhood of exceptionally nice, newer homes. In one of those houses, spacious and gracefully decorated for Christmas, the Alpha Garden Club gathered on the first Tuesday in December for its holiday meeting.

At this final meeting of the year, we were treated to a rare sit-down meal (chicken casserole, steamed broccoli, and the inevitable cranberry-walnut gelatin) with elegant service and lit candles in the shape of pomegranates floating in bowls in the centers of the tables. Everyone was pleased with the table decorations except Kate Brown, now a spunky ninety-seven years old, who was inspired by the candles to let me know just how much she despised that prissy Martha Stewart and all of her ilk. The talk was about the recent city elections and the "wonderful" concert by the Eaton Area Community Chorus held the night before at the old high-school auditorium. I hadn't attended.

My husband, Jon, had been brought up in New York City, the cultural capital of the country. Accustomed to world-class performers and living among what are arguably the most sophisticated and critical audiences anywhere, New Yorkers tend to scoff at amateur performances. Jon was particularly unforgiving about such things since he had been a performer and classical musician himself and generally decried the lack of taste in what he supposed was a vast cultural wasteland stretching from the metropolitan limits of New York all the way to

The Place Just Right

Los Angeles. I had automatically adopted his attitude when we married, especially since we were "in theater" and supposed to have more refined tastes than the masses. So I hadn't attended the Community Chorus concerts.

After the meal, the members of the Alpha Garden Club retired to the huge living room, festooned with wreaths and Santas, where chairs were arranged in a large semicircle around the fireplace. There was a piano in the far corner, and the gathering was colorful because the ladies were almost without exception wearing red and green for the occasion. I had forgotten about this custom, having spent holidays for the past thirty years in New York City surrounded by Jon's Jewish family. I showed up in brown and yellow.

At this point in the meeting, by convention, there would ordinarily be a film or a speaker connected with gardening, but in honor of Christmas, the committee had decided to present their own program using the "many talents found within the group." There would be singing and poetry reading on the theme of growing things. I began to get a little nervous. I knew that Jon, from heaven or wherever Jewish husbands go, was chuckling and trying to poke me in the ribs.

The program began with everyone invited to sing "The Holly and the Ivy" accompanied by Sharon Barnes of the Barnes Funeral Home. So far, so good. It was taken at a very brisk pace, not dirge-like at all, as I had feared. Although most of us were unsure of the words, when everyone sings together, it's not too bad. The general noise covers a multitude of sins.

Ruth Ann began the poetry reading (James Whitcomb Riley, "When the Frost Is on the Punkin" But before she read, she was lovely enough to mention my mother, sharing that after all these years, she still had the poetry notebook made in Helyn's class, still recalled poems and pieces of poems that Helyn had required them to memorize. That, of course, put all eyes on me, which made it impossible for me to make any facial expression except the most intense interest and appreciation. I had a sudden vision of Jon's spirit desperately trying to kick me under the chair.

I found, however, that once the reading actually began, I didn't have to act. I <u>was</u> intensely interested in James Whitcomb Riley to the point of being incredulous. I hadn't read anything about or by him for at least forty-five years, had even forgotten that "When the Frost Is on the Punkin" was ever a poem and not a saying. It lived up to all the clichés of sentiment and meter forecast by the saying itself. I admired that Ruth Ann kept it lively.

It was only the first of many readings that afternoon by several of the ladies. Most were culled from various collections of favorite poems, some from obscure magazines or newspapers, some all too familiar—all related to flowers, trees, or vegetables. There was even a poem announced as written by the poet Wadsworth. I took that at face value since so many of the poets were unknown to me. But when I heard the familiar words on daffodils, I realized we were hearing Wordsworth and that, perhaps, the reader misspoke, thinking either of Henry Wadsworth Longfellow (of which there were several examples) or Wadsworth Street, one block south of Main downtown. At that point I was sure Jon's ghost pulled my hair.

I hope, however, Jon's spirit hung around for a time, because had he left he would have missed something extraordinary. Something, I believe, even he, with his refined sensibilities, would have appreciated.

Somewhere in the midst of the afternoon program performed by the ladies of the Alpha Garden Club, perhaps even during the recitation of the poem by "Wadsworth," I happened to take my eyes off the reader long enough to notice the other ladies present. I was amazed to discover that whoever the reader, soft or loud, energetic or slow, the ladies in the audience were totally involved. Their eyes were closed, yet they were wide-awake. They were smiling and nodding, transported by the words, the images, the sentiments. Lulled and soothed by the rhythms, lost in the metaphors. If anything was missing in the skill of the reader, they were supplying it from their own inner voices. If the poet was lacking in sophistication or depth of understanding, they appreciated the message they received and did not judge. Furthermore, they were doing it together in the kind of communal experience all performance artists strive to create. By the time we got to the closing song, there was a warm glow in the room coming from more than the fireplace.

The song chosen was, appropriately, one of local origin—a Christmas song written by Ruth Lyons, for years a popular radio and television celebrity from WLW in Cincinnati. I remember her vividly from growing up in Eaton, where her daily talk show was inescapable. The song, "Let's Light the Christmas Tree," has a simple, even saccharine message. In the face of misery or evil, sadness and loneliness, the response must be to defiantly shine the light of love.

I thought of my mother, who had given the gift of poetry to many of these women in the first place. She had also, unknowingly, bequeathed to me my right to be there accepted without question by these people, sharing the memory of Ruth Lyons and her sentimental song as part of all our mutual childhoods in Eaton, Ohio. I knew they understood without asking that I, too, had urgent need for the light of love to be ignited in the face of sadness and loneliness. Suddenly, I was comforted to be there, in that room with the Alpha Garden Club, in the house across from Mound Hill Cemetery, in their hometown—and mine.

The hostesses of the Alpha Garden Club always send the members away with some sort of gift. Sometimes it is a small favor on a floral theme; often it is a plant. I came away from the Christmas meeting with a small poinsettia and a large piece of old-fashioned Christmas spirit delivered through the power and sweetness of a poem.

I intend to be in the audience for the next concert of the Community Chorus.

Time and Variations

The College Club of Eaton is another of the groups I joined after Jon died in order to keep active and involved in the community. On a recent Monday night, this club, which includes many teachers and former teachers, gathered at the home of one of its members for a meeting described as "back by popular demand." Most women I have met in Eaton love to read, and the program was based on a very simple premise. Each of us would bring a book or two we had recently enjoyed to share with the others.

Many of the books were novels; some new, most old. Hester brought ... *And Ladies of the Club*, my favorite novel about this region of Ohio. She thought she was getting a nonfiction book about a female investment club. Imagine her surprise when it turned out to be about small-town Ohio women who attended a literary club for half a century. She had found it quite moving. I thought it was unusually appropriate for this meeting.

There were a few political biographies and memoirs, some collections of inspirational readings, and two or three books on local history and crafts. I was the only one to bring science books—three books on human population genetics, to be precise. Jean, the wife of my former math teacher in high school and a good friend of my Aunt Ruth, implied later while driving home that the content of some of them bordered on controversial. Not that she minded, of course. It would be like me to do something different. I took that to mean I was my mother's daughter after all.

In truth I have, of late, become fascinated with recent discoveries in human population genetics. I sought out the books because of a pop-up ad that ran briefly on one of my genealogy websites advertising DNA testing to help "uncover your genetic past." Didn't I move here in the first place to reconnect with my past?

The books traced, by means of genetic testing, the origin and migration of early man over many millennia, and the mingling and dispersal of a variety of so-called races across the globe. When I had finished reading them, I was stunned. I felt my mind reshuffle in a way I hadn't experienced since college. Preconceived notions of genealogy and race, of cultural identity and nationhood, of heritage and ethnicity, came tumbling apart and reforming like black dots on a pair of rolling white dice. It seems to me that we are in the middle of a scientific revolution comparable—in importance and in its ability to change human thinking—to the revolutions begun by Darwin and his theory of evolution, or Einstein and his theory of relativity. Reporters should be shouting it from the satellite dishes on our rooftops.

Of course, these days, practically no one who isn't a scientist really takes such things very seriously in day-to-day life. There are large groups of people who, a hundred and fifty years later, still reject Darwin's theories out of hand as though they were just another opinion, no better or worse than their own. I don't understand people who reject knowledge because they don't like what it says. I love reading science books, particularly biology, although I have been known to pore over books in physics as well. I found in these genetics books a discovery process more thrilling to me than adventure fiction, more challenging than detective novels, more satisfying than romance.

I read *The Seven Daughters of Eve* by Bryan Sykes of Oxford University, which actually did, a few years ago, receive fairly wide press by announcing the discovery of the mother of us all. Dubbed "Mitochondrial Eve," this woman lived in Africa 150,000 years ago and possessed a certain sequence of DNA in her cells passed on to all women now alive. Along the way, of course, there were some changes (mutations) in the DNA—perhaps every twenty thousand years or so. Those variations eventually, over the millennia, defined the genetic composition in the same sequence of mitochondrial DNA for thirty-three other "Eves." Seven of those genetic sequences are found in 95 percent of the women in Europe. Thus, "the Seven Daughters of Eve."

Brenda Baumhart Mezz

On the inside back cover of Professor Sykes's book, in very small print, was an invitation to have my own DNA tested and, therefore, to learn which of the thirty-three daughters of Eve was my closest genetic mother. The seven from Europe were very well described from DNA samples obtained over years of research. The geneticists could speculate pretty accurately when and where these women lived and the migration pattern of their descendants. Having a fairly common WASP German/English family lineage, with nobody on my charts even remotely from any other continent, I naturally assumed my genetic mother would be one of the seven described in the book. So I sent for the kit, paid the rather steep fee, swabbed inside my cheek, and sent it off to Oxford, England.

After several weeks, the results arrived. To my astonishment, my maternal "Eve" was not one of the seven whose descendants constituted 95 percent of the population of Europe, but another one entirely, a woman whose descendants today are found principally in Iraq, Turkey, Pakistan, and Mongolia. They assured me there was no mistake. These discoveries happen every now and then, they said. Presumptions of ethnicity are never dependable when it comes to the genes. If my ancestors had more recently come from European countries, I could rest assured that at some point in history my "genetic mother" or one of her direct descendants had made "an exotic journey from the Levant to Europe."

I was incredulous. Iraq? American soldiers are besieged by terrorists every day in Iraq. My genes could hardly have come from a less popular place. I looked at Iraqi women on the newscasts sometimes caught rushing about the streets after a bombing, wailing, heads covered. I thought, "These are my genetic sisters."

How could that have happened? Maybe it was the Crusades, I figured. Some medieval English or German knight brought back a woman from Constantinople. Maybe she was a camp follower for a Magyar or Hunnish barbarian who rode along during one of the invasions of Europe. I will probably never, as long as I live, be able to trace my maternal family tree back far enough to solve the mystery, although I will, without a doubt, keep searching for clues.

The revelation to me from these scientists is that within the cells of my body, anyone's body, lies the key to the history of the entire human race. It is a coded message that geneticists have only recently begun to decipher. It is a message written in collections of chemicals, an alphabet of four letters, A, T, C, G, representing the four chemical ingredients of DNA and arranged in significant repetitions and sequences. Like the eight notes of an octave scale in music, like the circles, squares, and lines of the visual arts, like the meters and stresses of poetry, the hieroglyphs on stone tablets, the fragments of sound and inflection of human speech, the past comes back to us in bits and snatches—in infinite variation—if we are attentive enough to decode the signals.

I have learned that in the previous six hundred years (about thirty generations), I have had over a billion ancestors, not accounting for duplications, of which there were undoubtedly many. For instance, old Gilbert Fairbanks on my genealogical chart is my great-great (etc.) grandfather at least twice since different offspring of his many children (cousins many times removed) eventually found each other and married, leading by a convoluted path to me. I could say I have a double dose of genes from him, depending on the roll of the dice that happens when egg meets sperm. It isn't impossible I carry a gene or two from most of my ancestors, although genes are lost as heredity goes about its work of making new combinations in order to create human beings in infinite variety.

I like living in a body, indeed in a world, where pieces of the past appear in the present, where pieces of the present will reappear, in some form or other, years from now. It is a concrete physical connection to the millions of ancestors who came before—to Gilbert Fairbanks, to my Middle Eastern "Eve," to "Mitochondrial Eve" 150,000 years ago, and through her to the first living thing.

Feeling connected is very important, I am learning. More so the older I get. I like to know that in the final analysis, it isn't about me. It is about the process, however imperfectly we understand it. The scientists seem to be understanding it better all the time. At least the "how" of it. The "why" is another matter. The genes can't tell us that.

This is the season of the year in Eaton, and across the country, for high-school and college reunions. Joanne from my Saturday morning breakfast group has now been gathering materials from her high-school class in preparation for their fiftieth reunion dinner. She brought to the Eaton Place to share with us a copy of the *Eaton Eagle*, from 1954. Another fragment from the past resurfacing to play its part in some scenario—place and time unimagined by any of us fifty years ago. The kind of incident I have come to expect since I moved back to Eaton, Ohio.

Reading the yellowed pages, I noted that Betty Jane had tried out for and been accepted as a majorette for the Eaton High School band. As an eighth grader, I had made the honor roll along with Billy Joe Creech and Phyllis Hilbert. On the last page, in the corner, was a poem my mother had written along with a short profile on her career. The title was "Two Kinds of Tears." The idea was simple. Tears are for sorrow. Tears are also for joy. We need them both. I would not have understood that message from my mother in 1954. Now, having shed many tears of each kind, I received it with the love that brought it to me again across the years.

The past comes back in bits and fragments, snatches and pieces, motifs and shifting shapes. The past comes back wearing different colors than we remembered, dancing to different rhythms, playing in different keys and time signatures like the themes and variations of a Mozart piano sonata.

I came home to claim my own past. Now I know I will not die a stranger.

Acknowledgments

My now deceased husband, Jon Mezz, was the first person to encourage me to write a book like this shortly after we moved to Ohio. He shared that initial year of "confrontations with my past" and was also my first and possibly best editor. The book might have died with him, however, had it not been for the late Tom Mullen, retired Dean of the Earlham School of Religion (Richmond, Indiana) and founder of its Ministry of Writing Colloquium, who allowed me (a seeker, not a Quaker) into his advanced writing class. A classmate from my Earlham years, Tom took a special interest in this book and for months after the class ended tutored me in his home until the book was finished. I must also acknowledge the members of several writing groups with whom I shared much of this material and who are responsible for many revisions and fine-tuning along the way.

Thanks to the members of the "Memories to Memoirs" course offered by Miami University of Ohio and to our little Eaton Writer's Group, especially Ed Brooks, Tina Morgan, and Michael Gibbs, who gathered with me every Saturday morning at the Crosswalk Café to share writing and outrage at the state of the nation. I am also grateful to the members of my book club in Eaton as well as to the members of the Alpha Garden Club for their avid interest in this project and for prodding me to publish in spite of my trepidations. A special thank-you to Bill Grivna, my old and now new friend and fellow author. We shared our books in progress, and he beat me to the punch in getting his between covers. Thank you to Donna Levine for her outstanding and invaluable work copyediting the entire manuscript. And last but not least, a huge thanks to my son, David Mezz, for his love, help, and support.

About the Author

Brenda Mezz has spent her professional life either in theater or teaching, often both at the same time. She began and ended her career in high schools, teaching English, literature, composition, and public speaking—first in rural Ohio and last at San Fernando High School in the very urban San Fernando Valley in Los Angeles. In between she taught acting, theater history, speech, and writing courses in several universities, including the University of Minnesota, Wisconsin State University—Oshkosh, and North Carolina Central University. During those years Brenda appeared in, directed, or worked backstage for multiple community and university productions. She has degrees from Earlham College, Miami University of Ohio, and four years of postgraduate work in theater at the University of Minnesota.

In the late 1970s, Brenda was the stage manager for an off-Broadway production of *Diamond Studs*, brought to the Chelsea Theater by a repertory company in Chapel Hill, North Carolina. In Los Angeles she was assistant director for the Los Angeles Theatre Alliance, an arts service organization for fifty professional equity-waiver theaters, providing support in publicity, production, and management to its members.

Brenda retired back to Ohio in 2001 and began a new career as a writer. Besides her writing projects, she is heavily involved in local history, having facilitated, written for, and edited a history of Preble County townships in addition to other books, lectures, and presentations on the subjects of history and genealogy. She is a proud mother to her son, David Mezz, who is presently a magazine editor in Charleston, South Carolina. She is also a mother to four cats of which she is not so proud, but loves anyway.

Made in the USA
Lexington, KY
08 July 2018